MARRIAGE TO A PSYCHOPATH: THE AFTERMATH.

by

GLENN EDWARD KIRK

In memory of my late father Albert Edward Kirk.

For two of my granddaughters.

Georgina Milborne Swinnerton Pilkington.

Tamara Milborne Swinnerton Pilkington.

Fictitious names used where necessary as requested by my elder daughter.

MARRIAGE TO A PSYCHOPATH: THE AFTERMATH.

CHAPTER 1

A dejected and miserable little figure stood looking up at the towering stone archway, his heart pounding. He was close to tears.

"Dear God, please help me through this," he muttered, "God, why does it have to be me?" He looked back at the school road and saw his mother marching towards him.

"Glenn…Glenn…oh there you are my boy. Come on now, no tears please. We have to find out where we register." It was too much for him and as he fought back the impulse to want to cry, two tears dropped to his cheek.

"Mummy, why do I have to do this? I will be the youngest boarder in the school and the only boarder in my class. Please…PLEASE….take me with you."

Rose Kirk bent down to console her son.

"We have been through this all before young man. Your father clearly explained our circumstances and besides, we want the very best for you. St.John's is considered by many to be the best school in South Africa and you will quickly start enjoying all it has to offer. You will get used to it. Think on the bright side. No one at your age gets to see the world and enjoy experiences like you will be doing." She gently wiped away the tears, took his hand and they entered the stone arched entrance.

Rose and Albert Kirk had chosen to send young Glenn to boarding school at this early age for two main reasons. Firstly, he was an only child and, as such, they felt it imperative he learned to interact with other children on all levels but the second and most important reason was that his parents needed to be in Europe for a minimum of four months of every year. They could divide this into two annual trips but this did not fit in with the school curriculum. Boarding school was unavoidable.

In the middle of the Preparatory School quadrangle a young man sat at a table surrounded by files and papers. He stood up as mother and son approached him.

"Good Morning Ma'am, are you here to register your son?"

"Yes, I am young man. My name is Rose Kirk and this is my son Glenn."

"Very good," he replied as he looked down at his file. "Glenn I see you are assigned to Cullinan House. Your Housemaster is Mr. MacFarlane. If you follow those stairs up to the first floor, his office is the second door on the left."

"Thank you," replied Rose trying hard to conceal the rising anxiety she felt. The reality of her son leaving home at six years of age began to take hold and she began for the umpteenth time to question if this was in the best interests of her young son.

"What's wrong Mum?" croaked Glenn as they made their way up the well-worn stairs.

"Nothing my boy," she reluctantly replied. "It is all for the best and I am sure you will handle everything like a real trooper. You will, won't you?"

"Of course I will." He was determined not to show the desolation and hurt that tumbled around in his heart and the rest of his body. His stomach churned inside him.

Glenn Kirk was the youngest boy ever to be enrolled as a boarder at St John's. He felt lonely and helpless and knew deep down he had to do something about all the despair and pain that lay festering inside him. The weeks went by but matters did not improve. In fact, the situation deteriorated. His life was about to become a living hell. A fat slob of a boy, two years his senior named Williamson, together with two of his side-kicks, decided to take control of the newly registered six-year-old.

"You follow my rules and do as I say," Williamson screeched as he grabbed Glenn's tie, forcing him to grovel at his feet. It did not stop there. He pulled him back up and spat in his face. "Bugger off you little twit. Remember you belong to me!"

The taunting and bullying continued on a daily basis. Whenever his tormentors saw him they went out of their way to abuse and torture him both mentally and physically.

"Hey you, shit face," growled Williamson on one occasion. "Little mummy's boy has plenty of money I hear. Just remember anything you buy at the tuck shop you give us our share…understood?"

Glenn feeling strong glared at his aggressor but stopped at saying anything.

The inevitable happened. A few days later Glenn ran into Williamson and his two allies at the School Tuck Shop counter. Williamson was looking his usual aggressively ominous self. The Tuck Shop Lady noticed nothing.

"Good morning young man and what can I do for you today?" she asked. Glenn, his brain identifying various terrifying possibilities, decided he was not going to give these bullies the satisfaction of how much fear he harboured or how desperately their barbed verbal attacks penetrated his soul"

"One ice cream cone for me and one for each of my friends."

"Will that be all," she enquired as she handed over the cones.

He shot a quick glance at Williamson and hurried out of the shop.

Should he or should he not enlist the help of his mother was all he could think about as he ran back to the school building. Rose and Albert Kirk would be flying off to the UK at the end of the week and he knew if he was going to do something it had to be virtually immediate. He phoned his mother and gave a full report.

"Glenn do not say anything to your father. I will deal with those monsters." He was appalled at her reaction. All he had really wanted was her sympathy.

"Please…PLEASE say nothing!" Rose could hear the terrible distress in her son's voice.

4

"Very well but keep me updated."

"I will. I promise I will," he cried.

"If they carry on with this cowardly aggression they will have to be stopped," she retorted. Nothing further was said.

Glenn never once had trouble again. He knew his mother was a formidable woman but he had no desire to find out what she had said or done.

He still had bouts of homesickness and depression but slowly learned how to best control it. Whenever he felt the dark cloud of despair enveloping him, he reminded himself of how lucky he was to be at a decent school and, more importantly, free of the three terrible monsters. They eventually became a thing of the past.

"I can live with this", he would say to himself as he sometimes glanced anxiously over his shoulder. The foundation of a protective wall encircling his being had been laid, a wall that grew higher and stronger as the year went by. It would become his fortress in future years.

Sport was a number one priority at St. John's but Glenn had limited interest in cricket or rugby. Swimming was his passion. Those endless swimming lessons his mother had insisted on dragging him to were definitely paying off. He gained himself a growing reputation for the sport, so, he not being a particularly enthusiastic cricket or rugby player was not an issue. In addition to this he proved to be a promising pupil. His mother had also introduced him to horse riding but made the unforgiveable error of starting at four years of age. David Stubbs was enlisted and ordered to keep a close watch on her son. Unfortunately, one hot summer afternoon Glenn's pony decided to cool off with a roll in a nearby stream. He cried out for help but alas he, plus horse, tumbled into the water. His confidence was shattered. Rose reluctantly agreed to halt further lessons. He was delighted. It meant more hours drawing enchanting architectural plans and houses which he so loved doing. The great architect and creator of his school, Sir Herbert Baker was to be a lasting influence.

After the bullying nightmare was over Glenn's Prep School days blossomed and it was with a certain amount of shock he found himself preparing for Senior School, (St. John's College). The highlights of each year were seeing and spending time with his parents and often experiencing London and sometimes other European cities. Dreams of future possibilities were never too distant from his thoughts.

Included in his travels was a Musgrove and Watson School Tour of a number of European cities and other places of interest. His group of fellow travellers was made up of boys from St. John's, Michaelhouse, Hilton and Bishops. Some were to remain lifelong friends.

Finally, his last year at school came to an end and with it the reality of choosing a career path became a major priority. He had absolutely no idea what he wanted to do. An aptitude test at the University of the Witwatersrand did not really help but a possibility of a career in the legal profession was suggested. He subsequently enrolled at Wits majoring in Law and Classical Civilisations.

"I believe that is a good move my boy. It will also enable you to apply for a credit in Roman Law and possibly Constitutional Law should you study further in the United Kingdom," his father interestingly suggested. The seed had been sown although it had always been understood that there was a strong possibility he would go to an English University.

Glenn flourished at Wits. He made many new friends and a budding social scene developed. Having been 'locked up' in an all male boarding school for 11 years, it was considered not surprising, and the gender mix became much appreciated. There had been limited male/female interaction due to the school (St. John's) being literally over the road from Roedean, (an all girls school), but strict rules imposed by staff members of the two institutions prevented any sort of relationship developing.

It was during Glenn's first year at Wits that he and two close friends, Bruce Black and Willie Barlow, were invited by an American Mining Magnate to a small gathering at his Johannesburg home. The occasion was for his visiting daughter Sue to meet and make local friends. The Engelhard family was based in the States and also kept a rather fine house, The Court House, in Sandhurst Johannesburg. It was at this 'get together' that Glenn met Rachel, a Rhodesian/South African who had been living in London for the past three years. Her father Sir Frederick had recently returned to Johannesburg to join a highly reputable and respected Mining House. Rachel and Glenn had a spontaneous rapport and a warm friendship soon developed. She was not a student at Wits but was often invited by Glenn to join in at university extra mural events and other social occasions. She expressed boundless enthusiasm at these events and proved to be great all-around fun. She heard about Bruce and Glenn's impending holiday to Kariba in Zimbabwe (Rhodesia) and invited the two to stop off in Harare, where her family still had a house. She also invited a mutual friend, Anne Cowley, to stay for a few days and organised a small gathering in the family home for Glenn's twenty first birthday. After a happy birthday get-together Bruce, Anne, and Glenn made the long drive back to Johannesburg. Little did any of them know what the future was to hold for all three of them.

CHAPTER 2.

The few years at the Witwatersrand University proved to be a special time in Glenn's life. Unfortunately for him the end came too soon and plans had to be finally taken for a postgraduate degree in the United Kingdom. Albert Kirk invited his son for a one-on-one luncheon at the Johannesburg Country Club.

"Glenn, I believe it would be beneficial if you had a gap year between the two degrees." announced his father beaming fondly at his son.

"It sounds good to me," grinned Glenn.

"Very well my boy. I have given this much thought and propose that you slowly get exposure to our European interests. There is one condition. At no stage can you discuss or divulge any aspect or detail of our investments with or to anyone. DO YOU UNDERSTAND THAT?"

"I understand Father," replied Glenn in a controlled formal voice.

"There is more to this. I include your mother under this proviso. Naturally she has some insight into part of my business affairs but what she knows is very limited. You and I have built up a remarkable father and son relationship and it will continue to grow as the years go by. I have watched you mature and there is no doubt in my mind you are intelligent and capable enough to be part of it all."

Glenn sat still, a little overwhelmed by what his father had said. There was no doubt he felt an extraordinary closeness to his father even though their interaction had always been limited. His father had never hugged or kissed him. Any physical show of emotion had always been limited to a handshake. Albert Kirk was a typical Englishman of his era. Emotion was deeply in the heart but never easily displayed.

"Dad, you know I will never disappoint you or let you down."

"I know my son. You remember when you started boarding school and that horrendous child, Williamson, began his unacceptable programme of bullying and torturing you. I am the one who silenced him. My method of doing this had nothing to do with the school. I promise you I will always be quietly watching and caring for you."

"How did you do it?" blurted out Glenn.

"Not important but I warned his father of the consequences if his son continued."

"Did you know his Dad?" choked Glenn fighting back the tears.

"No, but I made the necessary enquiries…. I regard the matter as closed…. Let's get back to what we were talking about. It is time for you to familiarise yourself with our business associates in Germany and Switzerland. I have developed a substantially large business relationship with three major suppliers in these two countries and they are very keen for this relationship to continue growing. The two companies in Germany are BASF and Bayer, in Switzerland it is Ciba Geigy. All three of them have invited you to spend some time at their respective Company Headquarters. You will be their guest. Glenn you are being offered a massive opportunity at the highest level. I suggest you go to the Goethe Institute in Bavaria for a three month German Language Introductory course. It is especially designed for foreign students and is intensive. After that you will pretty much plan your own itinerary until your Law studies begin. My advice is you make good use of this."

"Dad, I cannot believe what you have just said! It has opened up a pathway to the future! How do you see my legal future? Should I still go to Cambridge? The entry Exams for Kings College are in a month's time."

"You must take the exams next month, but I am inclined to think you should qualify as either a barrister or solicitor as back up. Think about this. I have all the detailed information for you to set everything in motion."

Glenn did not wait for the Wits University graduation ceremony and after a few farewell parties flew to England in early December. Upon arrival in London he bought a new MGB sports car and set off for Bavaria Germany. Most of the proceeds from the two cars he had sold in Johannesburg gave him the liquidity to do this plus of course a little help from his father. The next stage of his life had begun.

The Goethe Institute was a totally new revelation. Students assembled from all corners of the world, North and South America, France, Spain, Portugal, Sweden and a few from parts of Asia. The branch of the school he had chosen was in Murnau, a village south of Munich near Garmisch Partenkirchen. Munich and Innsbruck were favoured weekend getaways, the former for all the amenities it offered, the latter for its skiing facilities. Every day became a total pleasure and his German language ability progressed well. During his stay he 'hooked up' with a fellow student, a striking blond American called Grace but he had absolutely no intention of a long term relationship. She was a determined young lady and liked to dominate and take control of all situations. It did not bother him, or so he thought!

"Glenn love, the course ends in two weeks. I see us taking a slow trip to England and then we should head direct to Los Angeles. You must meet my family and more importantly get to know my parents."

Glenn was appalled. He quickly pointed out her plan was impossible. He had commitments with BASF and Bayer as well as Ciba Geigy and all three had to be his priority. She was furious. After much discussion it was agreed his visit to the States would have to be later in the year. He never saw her again.

The itineraries from all three companies were special and very exciting. Glenn was enthralled. The duration of each visit was four weeks and the programmes all included introduction to management at all levels, luncheons, and general social gatherings. The weekends were to start midday every Thursday and end on the following Monday. The overall plan was to introduce to Glenn, their guest, some of the beautiful countryside and holiday destinations surrounding the pivotal headquarter areas. All accommodation expenses were to be for the host account, food and entertainment was generally young Glenn's responsibility. He was naturally delighted.

BASF Headquarters in Ludwigshafen were close to two vibrant cities, Frankfurt to the north and Heidelberg to the south. Frankfurt's art and cultural offerings thrilled Glenn. The museums and historic buildings enchanted him and the locals seemed to be eager to make every effort to respond to his questions and make him feel welcome. His inner architectural interest blossomed and his familiarity with various historical, and indeed, more recent architectural offerings, grew each day. He found the one weekend was too short and revisited the city for a second time the following weekend. He loved Frankfurt.

Glenn's next port of call was Heidelberg. He was totally captivated. Heidelberg had been virtually untouched by the destruction of World War 2 which meant it remained a town of immense charm. The views from each section were magnificent. Schloss Heidelberg perched on raised ground overlooked the entire place which beautifully added to the overall appeal of this town of learning. The atmosphere of Heidelberg University enraptured the young man and he made friends almost immediately on arrival. The few days he was there he enjoyed walks along the banks of the Neckar River and would end up in the Altstadt to meet new friends and sample the wonderfully decorated patisserie. It was a foregone conclusion that he would come back whenever possible.

Albert Kirk phoned his son, by prior arrangement, once a week.

"Hello Glenn, how are things going? Are you still enjoying yourself so much?"

"Wow Dad, I am sitting in this fabulous patisserie surrounded by out of this world delicacies. There are four of us sampling each other's initial cake choice so we are fast becoming cake experts! I wish you could see it all and be here. This must be the most beautiful University town on the planet." He hesitated and then added, "maybe I should register as a student here?"

"Forget about that," his father stubbornly replied. "A one year course of 'German Special' at Wits and a three month course at the Goethe Institute does not automatically make you fluent in German. Take the glamour out of the surroundings and face the reality Glenn."

"Oh, I know but it is an appealing thought." The subject was instantly dropped, never to be mentioned again.

The four weeks with BASF had spun by. It was time to move on to Bayer.

Bayer AG. Headquarters were in Leverkusen and situated on the banks of the Rhine River just north of Cologne. The administrative offices were in Cologne itself.

Glenn had visited Cologne on a few previous occasions and was enamoured with the Cologne Cathedral and its Gothic Architecture. Its size and grandeur never ceased to amaze him and his sometimes fertile imagination took him on impossible journeys to times far in the past. On each visit he spent time taking in the magnificently beautiful stained glass windows, some still surrounded by dreadfully damaged buttresses and walls. The Cathedral had been damaged in parts by air raids in 1944 as World War 2 was coming to an end.

"Dear God, you must have been instrumental in saving the greater part of this beautiful structure. For that, I and other Christians throughout the world, thank you Dear Lord."

Bayer originally was founded to manufacture dye stuffs but went on to produce solvents, resins, basic petrochemicals and fine chemicals. As with BASF, Bayer was keen to develop the relationship further. An extensive itinerary was once again organised for young Glenn. He seemed to have little time for anything but Bayer AG. After a few weeks he decided to take an early departure.

"Not so fast young man," his father said in a somewhat brittle voice. "Give it another week and I will explain to the Bayer management why you will be leaving early."

Eight days later Glenn was on his way down south to Switzerland, destination Basle. He was to be the guest of Ciba Geigy and Sandoz, (the two companies were only to merge in 1996 thus creating Novartis).

As with BASF, Ciba Geigy played host to Glenn for a four week period. Accommodation was once again included and Mr. Frei, the General Manager, took Glenn under his wing. The attention received was exceptional.

Basle is situated in the north west of Switzerland on the Rhine River close to the borders with Germany and France The river actually divides the city into two parts, the Ciba Manufacturing Headquarters in the industrial section of the north and the older commercial and cultural section in the south where Glenn was stationed. The strong local German dialect took him by surprise, but the brief anxiety receded once he realised everyone switched to 'high German' on hearing him speak the language.

"Glenn, it is a great pleasure to have you visit us in Basle", said Mr. Frei as the two met. "Your parents were very good to me when I travelled to both Johannesburg and London, on separate occasions of course. I had two marvellous dinners with your mother and father in both cities. It is my pleasure to reciprocate but more importantly to introduce you to our ever increasing range of products. Hopefully this will stimulate further growth between our two companies. Incidentally we want to show you what a magnificent country Switzerland is. Your father mentioned you had travelled within our borders before but I am sure a repeat visit to one or two destinations will not be a hardship. Am I correct in saying this?" He added chuckling to himself. "We will happily be responsible for all hotel expenses you might incur."

"Mr. Frei thank you so much. I sincerely appreciate your hospitality and kindness."

"It is our pleasure. He also mentioned you are enamoured with the Palace Hotel and St. Moritz itself so naturally we will include this in the final itinerary."

An excited young man phoned his father the same evening.

"Hi Dad, Mr. Frei is going out of his way to make me comfortable. I also have the use of a company flat for as long as I like. What do you think about that?"

"I think you are a very lucky young man. We have had a strong business relationship with Ciba for the last fifteen years and I am confident you will be well looked after during your time with them. By the way, I know you have two South African female friends attending Finishing Schools in Switzerland so it is an appropriate time for me to say, control the love side of things! You have more important priorities."

"Haha, I know I should have not told you about Grace!" laughed Glenn. "No need to worry about my priorities, I know exactly where they need to be."

The atmosphere at the Ciba Geigy Head Office encouraged interaction on all levels between Glenn and the company staff. He was accepted without question and the visit was a great success from beginning to end.

"Glenn, we are delighted with the strong interest you are showing in our products and services. How about taking a few days off to regenerate your brain cells?" Mr. Frei said encouragingly. "Have you anything or anywhere in particular in mind?"

"Have you any suggestions Sir?" quipped Glenn.

"Please call me Oscar. Yes, I have. One of my favourite spots is Zermatt. It is generally known for the excellent skiing it offers but with the spring/summer weather we are now experiencing, the snow might be a little thin up at the Matterhorn. May I suggest if that is the case you explore the lower mountains and villages. It is truly a beautiful area and a fantastic town."

"That sounds incredible Oscar. Thank you so much."

"I cannot let a member of my staff accompany you but I am sure your natural confidence will look after you." A few hours later Ciba Geigy confirmed his booking at the Alpenhotel and off he went.

Zermatt is almost completely surrounded by high mountains with a year round population of about 4000 people. Glenn arrived at the Jungfraujoch rail station, (Europe's highest station,) and immediately fell hopelessly in love with the magical village. He had been concerned about leaving his MG at a lower station parking facility but that was only a distant worry now.

The Matterhorn is a large near-symmetrical peak between the Swiss and Italian borders and is the highest winter sports area in the Alps and thus guarantees reasonable snow conditions all year round. Glenn thought he was up in Heaven. It is a ski paradise offering many gourmet restaurants, beautiful sun terraces and free ride adventure trails. The downhill trails are secured against all alpine dangers which seriously appealed to 'the moderate skiing ability' Glenn. There is no exposure to any risk of avalanche and is the perfect place to learn the art of free riding. He was in his element and with the help of a local ski instructor managed to withstand a couple of falls in the two days of skiing. Summertime hikers and skiers just share the mountain so he remained two more days revelling in the exhilarating beauty of his surroundings before returning to Basle.

The next weekend getaway was a trip to Interlaken.

"It is a fantastic base for seeing the best of central Switzerland's magnificent scenery. You can also enjoy superb lakeside comforts. I am sure you will have a wonderful time Glenn," said Oscar Frei beaming fondly at him.

"That sounds good. Thank you so much," replied Glenn without a moments hesitation.

"Incidentally, Interlaken is situated between Lake Thun and Lake Bernese. It is surrounded by the Bernese Alps. I suggest you take a train or cable from Interlaken station to get to the Jungfraujoch. It is there you will find the eternal snow that the Bernese Alps are known for. It is also an adventure paradise so enjoy!"

Glenn set off with eager anticipation. He had previously visited when he was much younger and had sampled the chic lakeside comforts that his parents so enjoyed. A cruise on the lake had been the most adventurous event of the five day holiday! It was now his time to be an adrenalin junkie and thrill seeker. After all, he was in an adventure junkies' paradise. River rafting was his choice. The first day was labelled as 'an introduction to river rafting' and he was prepared for a relatively gentle paddle. Nothing could have been further from his expectations! It was a day of extreme water rafting due to overnight hazardous weather conditions which left him cold, battered and with a harrowing fear that prevented him from taking to the water the following morning. He had quickly realised that despite his swimming prowess, it was not a sport for him...... so much for his reputation as a water baby! The experience had left him unsettled. He left to return to Basle soon after.

"Well young man how was your Interlaken trip? Did you enjoy it?"

Oscar Frei and Glenn were discussing his visit to Ciba Geigy in general and his travels in Switzerland in detail.

"It has been mesmerising Oscar and I want to thank you for your remarkable hospitality during my stay here. The whole exercise has proven to be a total revelation to me in all respects. I envisage a long term business association as well as a long term friendship relationship."

"What are your immediate plans before returning to the UK?"

"I have four months ahead of me of travelling around Europe with some business assignments that will require my special attention," replied Glenn. "My father will be joining me for a week or two and I am sure he has a lot planned for us."

"I spoke to him a few weeks back and he mentioned the possibility of a visit to Basle. I let him know our company flat will be made available to him whenever he should require it. I would also like you to know that you are welcome to use it for the next month should you require accommodation in this area."

"That is an amazing offer Oscar and I will definitely take you up on it."

"Excellent, then that is settled. I will advise our housekeeper accordingly."

CHAPTER 3.

'BUT IN A SHROUD OF SILENCE LIKE THE DEAD

I HEARD A SUDDEN HARMONY OF HOOVES

AND, TURNING, SAW AFAR

A HUNDRED SNOWY HORSES UNCONFINED,

THE SILVER RUNAWAYS OF NEPTUNE'S CAR

RACING, SPRAY CURLED LIKE WAVES BEFORE THE WIND.

SURELY THE GREAT WHITE BREAKERS GAVE THEM BIRTH.'

From 'Horses of the Camargue'   by Roy Campbell.

Glenn had first come across this poem in an English Literature class at St. John's College in his school days. He was immediately mesmerised and vowed to visit the Camargue as soon as he could. The time had come.

The Camargue is a little known region lying on France's Mediterranean coastline. It is part of Western Europe's longest delta lying between the Rhone River and the Mediterranean Sea. It spreads out much as a fan does and is like nowhere else in France. For Glenn the galloping white horses symbolised the wild spirit of the region and the personal freedom he had so passionately sought since starting school life. He had carefully researched the area and had decided on heading for Arles, an ancient Roman era town at the base point of the delta fan. His excitement increased as he saw each sign directing him onwards towards the Camargue. Finally, a sign pointed in the direction to Arles. He stopped his car, packed away the roof and sat in the sunshine marshalling his thoughts. He wanted his first experience of this enthralling countryside to be for him alone. He avoided entry to the town and followed a narrow road running towards the pink tinge of the horizon. Within minutes he became one with the grass filled marshes. The further he went, the rose coloured salt flats of the Camargue multiplied and continued to reached out to him as if to welcome him to the region and acknowledge his years of dreaming of the scenery that now lay before him. Glenn was in awe. He drove slowly making numerous stops, always calm and unhurried. This had to be a bird enthusiasts ultimate paradise. The pink hue became more noticeable the further he drove. He continued towards it's centre point. As he came nearer he felt he was entering another world. The teeming birdlife was beyond belief. Frolicking flamingos intensified the pink hue to the variations of colours and light. There was an array of species enjoying this, their natural habitat. The colour, the light, the moods were like nothing else he had witnessed in his life thus far. The fresh water, needed to complete the scene that lay before him, was supplied by the River Rhone, as were its partners, the sunshine and the ever reliable Mistral wind, all together in the creation of this magical kingdom. Evening was approaching but Glenn could not leave. He was in a trance. The changing depths of colour began to transform the early evening moods to reveal an unexpected sense of earthly drama. It was a sunset like no other he had ever witnessed. Then there was a gentle murmur as all the living creatures in the Camargue settled in for the night. A soothing peace eased him into a gentle sleep.

It had not been a comfortable night sleep for Glenn. He had woken up shortly after midnight feeling unsettled with too much on his mind. Eventually dawn arrived. He yawned as he stretched out his arms and stood up.

"I will have to go back to Arles and get some input on the white horses," he muttered to himself. He rolled up his ground sheet and packed up the car. The roof remained off. "I just hope I recognise the way back" he said out loud to himself as he looked up at the early morning sky. "Bloody Hell Kirk, you should have brought a compass." He drove into Arles three hours later.

Glenn was not in the Camargue to experience the culture of the region but when he came across two 'French Cowboys' in the town square he was intrigued.

"Yes Mr, our English not good but understand," quipped the elder one.

"Good Day Gentleman, I want to see White Horses of the Camargue. Can you tell me which way to go to find them?"

"We show you white horses. We give you horse to ride, us, $100."

"I don't want to ride a white horse," said Glenn with mounting agitation. "I want to see plenty white horses together."

"Yes Englishman, we show you plenty. We are guardians of Camargue Horses. Without us you see nothing." Young Kirk felt the resolve he had built up over the last sixteen years of not ever riding again, wavering.

"No galloping," he insisted.

"No problemo….when White Horses gallop, we gallop." This conversation was going nowhere. The dream of seeing and experiencing these majestic animals was receding. Glenn took control.

"Agreed, we go now." Within forty minutes three horses were saddled up and ready to go.

"Please be with me Lord"' cried Glenn wildly, his heart thumping uncontrollably in his chest, his mind a jumble of emotions. Realising the three of them were actually mounting White Horses of the region sent a thrill through his entire body.

"I can do this", he shouted as all three horses lunged forward. The reality of his dream had begun but nothing like this had ever entered his head!

They galloped into the morning sun and soon settled into a comfortable pace. Incredible landscapes were to be seen wherever they went. Rose coloured salt flats and grass filled marshes were the order of the day. There were multiple groups of birds on shimmering waters of small lakes and ponds. Then with great tenacity they turned southwards and trotted towards a huge flock of pink Flamingos. Nothing was disturbed. Never in his life had Glenn witnessed such natural beauty. He heard a shout, looked sideways and saw the one

Frenchman point eastwards. Within the haze was a group of magnificent white horses, far in the distance, splashing in the water. They danced and played. What a sight to behold! The three horsemen slowed down and as they got nearer, halted. It was like heaven on earth watching them play. Tears filled young Glenn's eyes.

"Thank you, thank you dear God, this has to be like no other place in the Universe." Seemingly without reason the horses stood still, motionless, and then without warning took to flight. The three horsemen dug their heals in and followed for a short distance at great speed before slowing down.

"Let them be," Glenn ordered. It had all been exhilarating beyond reason but chasing after them was unnecessary and damaging. The unbridled strength and wild beauty of the magnificent and magical beasts would remain with Glenn for the rest of his life.

'I felt part of their existence, part of their soul,' Glenn later told his father. 'It was one of the highlights of my life.'

As the sun began to set, the magic of the sky signalled the end of a truly great experience. His fear of riding slowly began to take hold once again, but leaving the Camargue was not an easy thing to do.

His muscles ached painfully from the intense exercise but he felt at one with the wilderness and freedom of the region. He also recognised his future lay elsewhere. He drove to St. Tropez.

Bridget Bardot had always fascinated him with her antics on and off the movie sets and modelling ramps but what had recently cemented his interest was her recent change of course. She had set up house in the hills behind St. Tropez and dedicated her life to animal welfare. He was no longer 'amused' by her, he was in awe of the actress. She had become an animal rights activist. Glenn booked in at the Sezz St. Tropez Hotel which was 200 metres from St. Tropez's beach and a short drive to Pompelonne Beach. He made enquiries about the French movie star. Found she lived a relative reclusive lifestyle and contact would be near impossible. He would have to arrange a meeting well in advance when he came to the town on a future visit. He subsequently chose to go to the famous topless bathing beach. Maybe beach relaxation would soften the aching stiffness of his muscles and joints. It was his first day in the town and the thought of topless women scattered around enjoying the sunshine somehow amused him. He rolled out his beach towel and tried to observe and relax. He soon lost interest and boredom set in. His mind was elsewhere.

During his South African University days Glenn had struck up a friendship with a fellow student, Chris, whose family kept a yacht on the Vaal Dam. Yachting weekends became the norm. It was tame sailing when compared to international deep water yachting but it had been most enjoyable. When the wind came up, quick thinking and excitement ruled. The medieval village of Grimaud (which has historical links to the Grimaud family) is perched on the hillside of the bay of St. Tropez and looks over a legendry setting and prime spot for a Marina. Property Developers and Investors got together and plans were drawn up for a state of the art Marina. Glenn heard about this and vowed to investigate further. Port Grimaud, lying 6km to the west of St. Tropez, was his destination. He set out on the coastal road and soon came across a large sign indicating a turn off to Port Grimaud. It didn't look too promising. The coastline appeared to be totally uninhabited. A simple hut was the only structure. Signage was all in French. He stopped in front of the unimposing prefabricated building, knocked on the door and entered. A robust bearded man greeted him in French and it quickly became apparent that the language barrier prevented any communication between the two of them. Glenn however did manage to gather that construction would be starting soon. He left disappointed and a little angry at the man's total incapability to supply information on the proposed new Marina.

"What a waste of time," he muttered, reminding himself he owed his father a weekly call. He looked at his map and headed east on the coastal route to Marsaille. He would phone his father from there.

"Hi Dad, great to be speaking to you. I did it! I found the Horses of the Camargue and guess what. I found the courage to ride again. They found it for me. It has been a momentous time, but more about it when I see you. How are you?"

"I am well Glenn. It is good to hear your voice and that all is going well. We need to meet up. I will be in Zurich on Thursday and have a meeting arranged which I would like you to attend. We can then spend the weekend together. How about St. Moritz?"

"Fantastic!" replied Glenn. He was eager to see his father and give him a detailed account of his exploits since they were last together.

Father and son duly met in Zurich on Thursday, completed all they had to do and set off for a long weekend break at the iconic Palace hotel in St. Moritz. Glenn had been at the hotel previously with his parents and was excited to be sampling it's incredible hospitality once again. It was his favourite hotel of all time.

His first visit was in winter and St. Moritz and surrounds had been a winter wonderland. He marvelled at being able to see the Cresta Run, a world championship bobsled run made of natural ice but regrettably did not get to try it out. The frozen lake over which the Palace hotel looked had hosted numerous winter sports during the visit, all of which had fascinated young Glenn as did the cosmopolitan lifestyle and blend of glamour of the season. It was a winter dream come true.

"Glenn, this time we are here to enjoy the pampering treatments, the hotel's bars and restaurants and above all, its legendary service. Let's spoil ourselves rotten! Your mother must be totally envious of us being together in such a breath-taking environment. It has a different atmosphere to what the three of us experienced last time. It is now summer which, incidentally, she prefers. For you and me any season will do! By the way, what are your plans for the rest of your stay in Europe?"

"I will spend some of the time with friends who were with me at the Goethe Institute and then my friend Tiki and I plan to travel to France and Spain as we slowly make our way back to the England. She is at a Finishing School near Lausanne at the moment and has another month and a half to go. We are both pretty excited about it. Should be a great trip."

"That sounds good but please, don't lose sight of your legal studies."

"No, she has to be in Cambridge a few weeks before my academic year starts so there is no chance of that happening. Dad, I am ready to start the next part of my life journey."

His father looked at him encouragingly.

"I think you will find stimulation and enjoyment reading law. You know I only want the best for you in whatever you do."

"Thanks Dad, I know you love me and I want you to know I truly love you."

This was the first time that father and son unreservedly displayed the great love they had for each other. Neither one would ever forget these precious few days at Badrutt's Palace Hotel in St. Moritz, Switzerland.

CHAPTER 4.

To be called to the bar in order to practise as a barrister in England and Wales an individual must belong to one of the four Inns in London. Of the four Inns of Court (professional associations for barristers and judges) Glenn had chosen Gray's Inn, the smallest of the four. He had been impressed by the buildings and gardens from the first time he had seen them and liked the history. Gray's Inn had been established around 1370 with full records dating from 1381. He enrolled and settled into the routine quickly. His subjects included Constitutional Law, Contract Law, Corporate Law and Civil Procedure. He had qualified for a credit in Roman Law. Albert Kirk had insisted that his son should reside in close proximity to Gray's Inn and suggested London House in Mecklenburgh Square, a mere two blocks away from Theobalds Road. Glenn was delighted with his accommodation and with the fact that there was no travelling time involved in attending lectures and other related activities. Time seemed to pass by at an extraordinarily fast pace both academically and socially and the end of his first year found him without plans for the annual academic year end, the June to August year end break. He phoned his father.

"Dad, maybe I could spend the holiday in South Africa?" he casually suggested.

"Glenn, your mother and I will not be in Johannesburg from mid-June. Remember it is the height of winter but you are more than welcome to spend the holiday period at the Hermanus cottage or in Johannesburg. Why not combine the two? There are, however, two requests I have for you during your stay. The first is that you visit Alexander Township and the second is you visit Baragwaneth Hospital. The hospital visit will introduce you to some of our staff members. I will say no more."

"Great," he responded with mounting enthusiasm. "That will be perfect. Winter in Hermanus is not ideal.....too wet and windy..... but possibly I can invite one or two friends for a week or two to join me there. I am thinking, as we chat, about stopping off in Greece on my way back." His father remained silent. Glenn quickly added, "that is if the airlines will allow a stopover at no extra cost!"

"Speaking of money Glenn, I think it is time for you to buy a small house in London. We can discuss it when I see you." Ten days later Glenn boarded a flight at Heathrow bound for Johannesburg.

Johannesburg in July is relatively quiet. His two friends Bruce and Willie were available most evenings but the hectic social atmosphere which they had all enjoyed so much was a thing of the past. They both had jobs, Bruce at the Johannesburg Stock Exchange and Willie in the family business. His other two great friends, Rick and Fuzzy were out of the country. This meant he found himself spending much of his time with Rachel which he thoroughly enjoyed. Things blossomed between them and a reluctance to say goodbye to each other developed. Things changed however as the departure date approached.

"You promised me you will be back in London before my sister's wedding so please don't forget it, Glenn." Her younger sister was to marry Michael, an ex-Guards Officer and the reception was to be held at the Guards Club in Mayfair London. Rachel reminded him daily about being at the wedding and it now had become an irritant for him. He capitalised on her anxiety, teasing her mercilessly about the Greek girls he was hoping to meet during his stopover in Athens and things soured. He brought forward his departure date from South Africa, hurriedly said goodbye and left. A monumental sigh of relief escaped his lips as the aircraft gained height and flew into the surrounding clouds.

"Athens, Hydra, Mykonos here I come", he said to himself, grinning devilishly.

Glenn held a special love for Greece. He loved the Greek laid back lifestyle, the architecture and of course the weather. He was a Backgammon player which brought him in touch with all things Greek! There was however one drawback, his culinary preferences like so many Englishmen did not include the local so-called delicacies. He had visited Greece on three separate occasions but never acquired a Greek palate. He stuck to plain old fried fish and chips when visiting the atmospheric harbourside restaurants and taverns. Spicy and oily Moussaka and Papoutsakia etc. were a no…no!

The plane touched down at Athens Airport late in the afternoon so it made sense to spend the night in a local hotel before setting off for Hydra. He was tired and chose a small hotel just off Syntagma Square, had thought about going to The Plaka for dinner, but settled for a small bistro type restaurant nearby. It turned out to be a superb choice as the food was good and international in flavour, the atmosphere enjoyably festive. It was a marvellous evening. He got to bed well after midnight.

The following morning Glenn not being a habitual alcohol consumer felt a little weak and squeamish. There was no way he could handle a ferry crossing to Hydra so opted for the flight to Mykonos. He just hoped his system could handle that! It did! He checked into the Mykonos Tagoo hotel and vowed to enjoy a quiet and relaxed few days on the island, one of his favourite holiday destinations of all time. Mykonos meant calm and relaxed times which included fun times. Glenn's first three days and evenings were of the calm and relaxed variety, the fourth something a little different. He dined at a quayside restaurant after which he strolled along the water edge viewing some of the yachts.

"Hey mister, come up and join us for a drink. We need company!" It was a casual friend he had come across a few times at The Saddle Room, a club in Mayfair London.

"Great to see you Myles," he retorted as he hopped onto the deck. "What brings you to Mykonos? Stupid question, you obviously sailing around the Greek Islands."

"Yeah Mate, two glorious weeks on the Aegean Sea. Couldn't ask for more than that, and you?"

"Been in South Africa for the last two months and am on my way back to London."

Myles introduced Glenn to his three yachting companions, handed him a beer and promptly said.

"We are going to check out the clubs tonight. You have got to come with us."

"Would love to," said Glenn without a moment's hesitation.

An hour later all five of them were on the dance floor showing off the latest London dance moves. It was the height of the season in Greece and the club speakers were thudding and thumping with the beat of the music. People danced with partners, people danced alone. The vibe was amazing.

"Hey Myles, this is like New Year's Eve," shouted Glenn.

"Every night here is like New Year's Eve," screeched Myles. There was no point in trying to talk. The music drowned everything. Glenn's eye caught the image of a blonde girl rhythmically dancing towards him. He liked what he saw! They danced together for a few minutes, she powerfully moved into him, their lips met, their tongues consumed, and she was gone. He had had enough, said goodbye to Myles and company and returned to his hotel. Glenn only discovered back in London that she was one of the Onassis Party on the island that night.

Rachel had arrived in London a few days before Glenn's return and was caught up in the rush of last-minute wedding preparations. They only had access to the main public room three hours before the wedding reception began so organisation to the smallest detail was a must. Sir Frederick, the bride's father believed he had to be in control of all proceedings if it was going to be a successful occasion and rapidly irritated the entire Guard's Club staff. Matters worsened and it was touch and go as to whether the reception would take place at all. A Committee Member of the Club, an old Guards Officer himself, finally had to insist Sir Frederick leave the building and at last all plans and proceedings fell in to place. Mary and Michael were officially married, both beaming from ear to ear, a remarkably happy couple, and their guests enjoyed a wonderful reception. It was at the wedding that Sir Frederick took Glenn aside.

"Well young man, what are your intentions with my daughter?" Glenn was shocked. "Must I arrange a wedding for the two of you?" Glenn hesitated, then calmly replied.

"Not yet sir!"

Rachel returned to Johannesburg and her job as a Montessori teacher, Glenn submerged himself in his legal studies and his life in London.

Glenn had always loved London. It remained his city of choice throughout his life even though later on in his life he spent little time there. As a student he thrived on the sights, sounds and smells of this magnificent metropolis and the stimulus to gather knowledge and to experience all the enjoyment, was ever present. He was later to live in New York but London would always remain his special place. There was however one thing worrying him. Was he ready to make a commitment in marriage? Three months later he phoned Sir Frederick.

"Sir, may I have your daughter's hand in marriage? I want to marry Rachel."

"That sounds very formal Glenn, but it is the way I like it to be. My wife and I give you our blessing. It will be an honour to have you as our son-in-law."

"Thank you, Sir, I will be phoning Rachel tonight to propose. Please don't let her know anything about my telephone call." He hung up.

"Rachel, my love, I have a question for you. Will you marry me?"

"Yes….yes….yes, of course I will. Make it soon. I cannot stand waiting any longer." She had accepted and Glenn duly selected photographs from the latest DeBeer's diamond ring exhibition in London. He chose the three he liked most and sent them off to Johannesburg. Rachel decided on her favourite design and the picture was sent to Sidersky Jewellers to be manufactured. Albert Kirk then handed over the ring to his future daughter in law. It was an easy painless procedure for all concerned even though the cost was a little more than Glenn expected.

Glenn touched down in Johannesburg a month later. The wedding was scheduled to take place in five days. Two groomsmen accompanied him on the flight, the others were all South African friends. The five days seemed to be one long social whirl, dinners, drinks and of course the signing of the prenuptial agreement. They were both twenty-three years of age with some assets and Glenn owned a property in Barnes London. Rachel's financial position was unknown but like Glenn and his father, she also received a monthly allowance from her father.

Finally, the wedding day arrived amidst great excitement and last-minute attention to detail. Brief panic set in when it was discovered the mother of the bride's hat could not be found. It had supposedly been sent from Paris a day earlier but a quick call to the courier sorted it all out. It had been delivered to the wedding venue and not the family's Johannesburg apartment.

The wedding ceremony was very special for both of them. It was held at St. Mary's Cathedral, a Romanesque style building designed by Sir Herbert Baker and situated in the middle of Johannesburg. This created a logistical nightmare for Sir Frederick particularly with the timeline allowed but, somehow, he managed to pull it off without any major disruption. All the guests, (three hundred of them), managed to travel safely from the Cathedral to the Reception venue, The Johannesburg Country Club. The bride's father's organisational skills were exceptional and everything went according to plan. Rachel positively glowed and nothing could possibly take the smile from her enraptured face. It was a day to be forever remembered. That night they spent at a family's Magaliesberg farm and the following morning the couple boarded their flight for Marrakesh (via Spain) and the La Mamounia Hotel. They enjoyed four magnificent days in the city and then moved on to Milan where a new motor vehicle awaited them at the Alfa Romeo factory. The next stop was Glenn's dream place, the Palace Hotel in St. Moritz. He wanted to give his new wife a honeymoon that she would never be able to forget. Then a slow trip, via a much more built-up Port Grimaud, to London, back to post graduate studies and a new life as a young married couple. The perspective had changed a little but the thought of London as the city of fun and laughter remained. Rachel developed an ongoing habit of calling out to her new husband "I love you Glenn". It became a laughable catch phrase and added to the newness of marriage. It was exciting and wonderful to behold. They loved married life!

Glenn had brought in builders to do a few alterations to the house which were completed a few days prior to their return to London and suggested shortly after this a casual evening at home with six of his student friends.

"Rachel darling, I have invited six of my student friends for drinks and snacks on Friday. I want you to meet them." She pouted ever so slightly.

"Do we have to have them so soon? I only want to be with you" she cried. He was taken aback, hesitated and chose to ignore her reaction. The six friends came to the house and Rachel was the charming hostess he had always admired. The evening was a great success.

The weeks went by and the couple found themselves happily settled in a comfortable domestic routine. Marriage was enjoyable and pleasantly satisfying. During the next few months Rachel's father and mother made a two week visit and the four of them enjoyed some of London's finest restaurants and attractions. Sir Frederick believed himself to be a top gourmet expert. He certainly looked the part and his choice of restaurants was superb. His manipulative demeaner he was known for disappeared and he proved to be a jovial and contented father-in-law. Eventually it was time to say farewell and they returned to South Africa.

It was a few weeks later that Glenn noticed his wife's developing disquiet and increasing moodiness.

"Rachel my love, you have so much time on your hands, why not take in some of the vast cultural delights London has to offer. It is three years since you lived here so get back into that investigative and fun mode you used to so enjoy."

"I have no friends here who can join me. All my friends are in Johannesburg and besides, I love you and only want to be with you," she whined.

"You have sisters here. Ask one of them to suggest something and the two of you can go and have a good time."

"NEVER....Petra spends her day running her children around, and Mary is too busy socialising. We do not have the same interests," she mumbled, then hesitated and finally said, "Let's start a family." Glenn was speechless. Not in his wildest dreams had he expected this.

30

"Rachel that is a wonderful thought but not in the least bit practical at the moment".

"Why not," she snapped back sharply. "You are so involved with your student life and I have nothing. You study all day long and ignore me. This is not the life I want."

Ten months later found Glenn and Rachel in panic mode.

"Where is my blue bag? Find it immediately. Oh, dear God I cannot wait. Just get me to the hospital. Glenn help me.....I am so frightened."

Hannah took twenty-four hours to make her appearance. The pain was unbearable and an epidural became necessary, but in the end the baby girl was greeted with absolute love. The father adored his little daughter, the mother took another twenty-four hours to bond.

"Mr. Kirk, this lack of empathy and love for the new born is quite normal and common place after an epidural. All will be well." Rachel became a totally entranced mother and, once she was home, also a devoted and loving one. Within a few days everything settled. The two new parents were aided with the responsible and uncomplicated help of a full-time nurse given to the young couple by her parents, initially for a two week period and then a follow up refresher period of another two weeks. It was appreciated by them both but when it was time for Nanny to finally leave, they felt it now was their turn to look after Hannah permanently. Rachel and Glenn had entered the next stage of their lives, parenthood. The wonder of their little daughter was enthralling and attending to her each day was a total joy. There was however an occasion (or more of an incident) that nearly threatened the end of the marriage.

Princess Margaret and her husband Anthony Armstrong Jones were to have dinner at Gray's Inn. It was a custom for enrolled students to 'eat dinners' four times each term. The High Table was reserved for the two guests and other dignitaries while, at the Lower Tables, students in groups of four followed the tradition of toasting the Queen and Country before each serving. Port was the order of the ceremony. It was an honour to have the two diminutive Royals attending and a controlled but enjoyable atmosphere prevailed. When the time came for the Princess and her husband to depart, Glenn and a few of his mates surrounded the royal car and cheered as it was started up and slowly moved forward. Princess Margaret panicked and must have urged the driver to accelerate. By this time more students had joined the group as they over eagerly pushed the vehicle from behind. Glenn would never forget those two white and worried faces peering through the back rear window as the car sped out. Nothing further was ever said about the incident. The result of all this was boisterous celebrations in Soho. Time was not of the essence and Glenn pulled up at his front door in Barnes shortly after 2am. The house was awash with lights as were other homes in the street. Rachel was in total shock. She had called the police while other residents phoned hospitals and all emergency centres. Glenn's friend Charles was sitting at the front door as he got out of the Alfa. Charles had also been at the dinner.

"Bloody Hell Glenn, where the hell have you been? Your wife is in an uncontrollable state. You are in a shit load of trouble…. good luck mate." He got up and left. Glenn simply looked at the dark green front door, felt dreadful guilt and walked in to face his distraught wife. She looked at him as though she has seen a ghost.

"Where have you been?" she screeched. "I thought you were dead." She ran forward and grabbed her husband, tears rolling down her cheeks. "How can you do this to our baby daughter. How can you do this to me?" Glenn knew he was in serious trouble. She turned around and ran up to the bedroom and locked the door. It was two days before he was allowed back in again.

It took Glenn another year to realise he had an emotionally immature wife who was also a remarkably adept manipulator. He was about to enter pupillage but his wife's constant moaning about most things in general but more particularly about her lack of friends and no support system in London, made him realise that if his marriage was to continue, he had no alternative but to pack up and move to South Africa. A month later they boarded a flight at Heathrow, destination Johannesburg. Their new Neo-Georgian house in Wimbledon was let, the car and other personal belongings followed by sea.

CHAPTER 5.

"Glenn, my boy, are you sure this is what you want to do?"

"Yes father, I feel I need more exposure to the Corporation life in general and more particularly to financial management and investment structures".

"I agree wholeheartedly, but the final decision must be yours".

Glenn had been offered a job as a management trainee at the Head Office of a large Mining House based in Johannesburg. His father-in-law had, in some way, been involved in his capacity as an Executive Director of the Company.

"Don't worry about the salary as I expect only a minimal will be involved. I will subsidise some of your living expenses and I believe your immediate priority is to find a family house. You cannot stay with your father and mother-law indefinitely. How long is Lady Robson to remain in Rhodesia?"

"She is there until we find a house, so I expect three months."

He looked kindly into his son's eyes. "You have your work cut out for you if your marriage is to survive. Rachel is a very complex and troubled young lady". Glenn did not reply. He hoped and prayed once they were settled things would improve.

The young family settled into Glenn working and Rachel caring for their new born baby. For Glenn it was essentially working in a corporate world while for the two of them it was a continually escalating social scene. They developed a widening circle of friends and the future looked promising. Glenn Edward Kirk took to corporate life with enthusiasm and resolve finding it enjoyable but also very challenging. The young management trainee sector demanded relatively long hours and much interaction at a social level. Rachel proved to be a major asset and as the month's passed they found they were in great demand. She loved the popularity and her ability to show great enthusiasm for all things stood them well. Yes, they were both happy and the future looked promising. Promotion for Glenn came a year later when he was chosen to be a personal assistant to Mr. Damian Hetherington. Herrington was an Engineer, a brilliant negotiator and this, together with his entrepreneurial skills qualified him to run the Industrial Division. Glenn's job was to ensure everything operated smoothly in the office, to prepare for meetings and, most importantly, to learn as much as he could. He thrived in the environment. Hetherington also had an additional office staff member, an African/Indian called Jackson who fascinated young Glenn. He was an affable chap but there was more to him than was generally believed. The fascination came from his extraordinary ability to observe and retain a great depth of knowledge regarding Industrial matters. Glenn wanted to get to know him better.

"Rachel darling, there is a colleague of mine you should meet. He appears to have extraordinary talent and I would like the three of us to have dinner here at home one evening."

"Do not be ridiculous. You will only embarrass him," she retorted.

"I genuinely believe he is hugely capable and will open up in a comfortable atmosphere."

"Absolutely not," came her determined and rapid reply.

"Very well, I will invite him out for a drink after work and take it from there."

"You are wasting your time."

Glenn and Jackson got to having a drink together but it was felt by both that there was a lack of satisfaction and enjoyment in each other's company. Glenn was disappointed. He put it down to the uncharacteristic situation of black and white ethnic groups not openly socialising in public. He felt sad and blamed himself for creating a situation that only took 'his white security' into consideration, a security in an unjust society that afforded him privileges built on vile prejudice and enforced by a fanatical government that manipulated Christian beliefs to suit their ultimate aim of total oppression of all who were not Caucasian. It had been so different at Gray's Inn. It also worried him that his wife appeared to regard herself as special and, in some way, unique. He could see she felt she could only be understood by, or associate with, others who were considered special or were high status people. Glenn began to notice with concern that she loved being the centre of attention, loved talking about herself and her accomplishments, and, above all, was extremely sensitive about maintaining her idealised image of herself.

"Dad, I am a little disturbed about certain matters concerning my wife. I have no idea as to what I should do."

"My boy you have to try and help her but it is not something I can get involved in. I noticed from the first time I met her that she has a sense of self-importance and possibly exaggerates her achievements. She expects to be recognised as superior and her attitude needs to change but be careful and be gentle."

"I will try," he grunted, reluctantly agreeing something needed to be done.

The workload increased and Rachel continued to be part of their increasing Johannesburg circle. It was a few months later that Glenn once again became aware of the deepening neurosis in his wife. Her social life was paramount. Any intrusion on this was not allowed.

His wife's sister, Mary, and her husband had recently moved to South Africa, a move that was essentially a business transfer. Michael was an old Harrovian, had initially joined the Guards after leaving school, subsequently went out to Rhodesia, (Zimbabwe) and joined the police but, shortly before his marriage to Mary, changed careers and was accepted by an insurance company operating out of London. The official reason for the African transfer was to see how the Durban and Johannesburg branches operated within a much smaller market structure. It was understood by Glenn that it was purely a manipulation on behalf of Sir Frederick to have his daughter near her parents, especially her mother who adored her. Michael was not an entrepreneur, and it was reasonably obvious the career choice was unwise but, regrettably, he had little say in the matter. Within weeks of their arrival the reality of Rachel's feelings towards her sister took hold of the young Kirk household. A fiery jealousy surfaced in Rachel. Glenn, who was an only child and had never witnessed or experienced sibling rivalry to this degree watched helplessly as depression festered within his wife. He tried reasoning with her, but all his reassurances fell on deaf ears. Finally, the situation reached a climax point as invitations were sent out by Mary to most of Glenn's and Rachel's friends. The party was to celebrate Rachel's birthday.

"She wants to take over my friends," screamed Rachel in a violent rage filled with anguish.

"Come on Rachel, friends that become cool towards us are not worthy of our friendship and loyalty. Friendships are special and I guarantee you will enjoy your sister in your social circle."

"NEVER!"

They went to the party and it was a huge success. Glenn watched her interacting with everyone for much of the evening and could not help thinking her superficial charm, coupled with her rather arrogant demeaner, was troubling. Who was this woman whom he called his wife?

They got home around 1.30am, checked in on little Hannah and went to bed. Within an hour Rachel was having violent convulsions and uncontrolled diarrhoea spells. Glenn carried her to the bath, trying to help and clean her in any way he could. Doctor Lawrence, the family General Practitioner was called and despite the time immediately came. He conducted a thorough investigation and his diagnosis was simple. Extreme stress and emotional trauma resulting from severe anxiety and jealousy regarding her sister. He injected a strong tranquiliser into her backside.

"Doctor is this going to be an ongoing problem?" enquired her husband.

"Glenn, she is going to need a lot of support from you. There is much more to this than just jealousy but maybe she will overcome it on her own. I do not know if you want to consult with a specialist as to what should be done, so let us wait a little longer and see what happens."

"I do not think there is any point in seeking professional mental help at this stage. I will watch her closely and try and avoid similar situations occurring."

The next morning it was as if nothing had happened. Glenn convinced himself it was a one-off fit spurred on by jealousy and put the matter to rest.

The Kirk's social whirl continued with Glenn having to manage his ever increasing workload as well as the enormously busy social calendar. In the midst of all this he started having doubts about the woman he had married. This constantly played on his mind. Added to this Rachel suddenly announced it was time for them to have another baby. He was naturally delighted but more particularly so in the hope it would be a son. Rachel and Glenn's second child were born in Johannesburg weighing 7lbs.10 ounces, a little girl named Alexa. Both parents were enraptured with their new born baby.

"Two down, one more to go," he laughingly announced to his wife.

"I am not going through that again," she angrily retorted before bursting into tears.

"Do not worry sweetie," said the nurse as she entered the room, "the hormones will settle down."

"How long?" whispered Glenn.

"It varies from patient to patient and is quite normal. There is nothing to worry about."

"Maybe I should get professional help," thought Glenn as he reminded himself of Dr. Lawrence's words on the night he had called the good Doctor in to attend to his wife. He decided against it but slowly doubts about the woman he had married once again played with his mind. He had originally believed he had married a fascinating attractive woman filled with laughter and amusement. He had, in fact, married an overbearing vacuous girl living in a cocoon of little consequence and total foolishness. Her bad spelling ability and limited vocabulary worried him and he began to see her grasp of reality was non-existent. Her reading intellect extended only to Barbara Cartland novels which precluded any intellectual opinion and discussion on most subjects. He had to admit his image of her had radically changed. She typified the silly female whose life revolved around lady's afternoon bridge and weekly tennis parties. Added to this was her earnest desire to be seen at all so called society gatherings. When some such invitation was not extended, her husband had to deal with her nervous neurotic episodes and uncontrolled bouts of depression. Not a home environment conducive to romance or any form of domestic fulfilment. He had originally presumed he could influence her towards a more intellectual and fulfilling life but now began to accept that all it was, was an idle dream. He also now saw an innate stubbornness and intolerance within her coupled with an indestructible selfish approach to all matters involving her lifestyle. All he could do was hope and pray that this child would help to make matters better.

Months went by with little disruption. "Glenn, darling, I think I need more stimulation in my life. I am surrounded by people who do not appreciate me or understand my motivation in life."

"And what is that motivation my dearest?"

"Why of course it is my ability to lead. I have so much more in me than people realise, and I think my starting a small Montessori school is the way forward for me. Nothing big, merely four or five children. What do you think?"

"I think it is a brilliant idea. Will you do it from home? Perhaps convert the garages into a school area."

"Yes….yes…..that is what I will do!" Suddenly she switched into a business mode. "I will make my own Montessori equipment and I already have an idea who I will invite to join my class. They will naturally be paying pupils. My background and expertise does not come for nothing!" She continued to gush and gesticulate on her Montessori plans. Glenn supported and encouraged all she had to say. He prayed this would give more meaning to her both mentally and physically. It began to look very promising. His one inner concern was that she had only done a one year course. He however, sincerely hoped it would be enough instruction to run her own Montessori school.

The final pupil choice was by invitation only and, without any glaring preference, the five chosen promptly arrived at 9.00am on their first day. Included in the selection was little Hannah, the love of her father's life. He marvelled at her joy and excitement as she and her mother greeted each pupil as they arrived.

"Maria Montessori, maybe you are going to save this marriage," Glenn muttered under his breath.

"Glenn, are you going to join us on our first day?" enquired Rachel.

"No, my love, I think give it a little time for everyone to settle down and I will call in then".

It was two months before he visited the little Montessori kindergarten school.

"Glenn, I am still waiting for you to see how good my school is," announced Rachel one morning as he was leaving for work.

"I am so sorry but everything has been hectic at the office. I am part of a new project but your timing is good as tomorrow for me is relatively free, my love. How about I sit in a corner and watch all the interaction," he happily suggested.

"Tomorrow is perfect. I will call you in once the day has started. This is so exciting and I know you will be hugely impressed."

Glenn was up for his early morning swim but Rachel was nowhere to be found. Sure enough she was in the classroom doing a last minute touch up before school started and Glenn came in.

"Lucky children having such a dedicated teacher," he said smiling as he walked in.

"I want everything to go smoothly for you so am making last minute changes. I want everything to be perfect," she announced.

"I have absolutely no doubt of your capabilities my love. Please just treat it like a normal day," he replied encouragingly. She briefly turned around, smiled and went back to her fidgeting and moving things around. Glenn could see a car entering the driveway. "I will be back in thirty minutes".

"Good morning children, we have a visitor who will be arriving very soon. He is my husband and Hannah's father. I have told him how clever you all are and he is very excited to see what we do. Is that good news?"

"Yay...yay...yay", came a rather raucous reply with the clapping of hands. There was a knock on the door and in walked Glenn. The pupils were enthralled and immediately stood up and greeted him.

"Morning Mr. Kirk, we are so pleased to see you here," came the eager response.

"Good morning, everybody, I am delighted to be visiting your Montessori School. I will quietly sit here while you carry on with your class." He pulled up a chair and sat down, participating where he thought he could, making sure he was not creating any disruption. About 40 minutes later he again addressed them all and left.

That evening as Glenn drove up to the house, he realised he had to be frank about the brief morning visit. "Control yourself Glenn," he mumbled softly to himself. "Be tactful, be honest and definitely not critical." He entered the house. Rachel heard him and called out.

"Hello darling, I will be down in a minute." He went into the drawing room and headed straight for the drinks tray, He poured himself a scotch, downing it almost immediately. Alcohol was not a favourite of his and clouded thoughts were not an option. Rachel walked in, at first smiling, then with a little concern.

"You do not look too good. Had a rough day?" she asked and not waiting for a reply added, "So what do you think of my Montessori School? If I say so myself, I have achieved wonders in setting it up in such a short time. I guess it is the wonderful training I have received in London."

"Rachel dear, I do think it is remarkable what you have achieved. You have done an incredible job but I am a little concerned about how strict you are with those tiny children."

"That is absolutely ridiculous. A firm hand is needed for security and understanding. Montessori is all about security in what they are doing while at the same time doing what each child finds it wants to do."

"I understand but is it really so necessary to be so firm with them?"

"You have to be strict to have security. I should know. I am the one who is a Montessori Directress."

Glenn decided to say no more. He personally felt she was exaggerating her achievements as far as Montessori was concerned and, furthermore, he was left uncertain as to what extent her so called talent affected her general behaviour. What also disturbed him was her unfettered determination to feel special and in control. Did this cover up feelings of insignificance and defectiveness? He brushed aside his thoughts and carried on with life. Two months later the little school hit a serious bump in the road. One of the pupils, a delightful little girl of a very good friend told her mother she was not happy at the school and asked to leave. Rachel was quietly furious. She could not help herself. She loved to be the centre of attraction and now felt an anger that her presence had been ignored.

"Rachel, do not say anything to the mother. Be reasonable and show disappointment that her daughter will no longer be benefiting from your knowledge and understanding of Montessori. Leave it at that."

"I suppose you are right, BUT, she really should be made to understand how lucky she is to have me as her teacher. It is not for me to explain this to both the mother and daughter. It is not for me to consider her needs. She must toe the line and do what I say."

"I understand how you feel but in the interest of peace and good-fellowship, let it be. Just leave it at that." Glenn breathed a sigh of relief. Hopefully it was all over. He vaguely understood her need for excessive admiration and thus her reaction to the situation but hopefully all this was a thing of the past.

Regrettably the school closed down four months later. Rachel claimed it was simply not a financial proposition. Glenn knew she was preoccupied with fantasies of unlimited success in life and the school could never fulfil this.

CHAPTER 6.

Life in Johannesburg progressed. Hannah was growing and little Alexa was an enormous joy for the two parents. The elder daughter was placed in a school called Kingsmead and the younger, little Alexa, remained with her nanny so as not to be a burden for her mother. Rachel appeared to be a very good mother in all respects, with the exception of being extremely socially involved with a group of like-minded friends. Glenn allowed himself to relax. He was a little concerned about her busy lifestyle, tried to encourage more of a charity dominated existence but quickly realised any charity work was of no interest to her whatsoever. Perhaps he had not fully appreciated the strain of motherhood on a young and socially preoccupied mother. The fact however soon became apparent that she totally lacked empathy with others. He noticed she was unwilling to recognise or identify with the needs and feelings of others and, added to this, had a crippling thirst for attention. Glenn had absolutely no idea of what to do. A strange thought sometimes entered his mind. He would keep the marriage afloat until young Alexa's eighteenth birthday. Only a few years later did he fully realise how ridiculous such a thought was. Yes, marriage was definitely not what it was made out to be.

Alexa came of age for Kingsmead and off she went. She idolised her sister and the ever loving Hannah made every effort to include her in what she did. Hannah was a very popular young lady and most certainly was the apple of her doting father's eye. Alexa appeared to follow in her mother's footsteps. He, however, loved both his daughters. Rachel was different. She continued to be occupied with fantasies of unlimited success in everything she did or wanted to do and gave an impression of believing she was always exceptionally well dressed and extraordinarily beautiful. Glenn now saw that these fantasies were a way to fend off inner emptiness and to feel special and in control. It was actually quite extraordinary the ends she would take to avoid feelings of insignificance and defectiveness. He began to ignore her. It was a relatively easy thing to do and a simple way of handling an otherwise frightening situation. There was one thing he did watch with utmost care and scrutiny. It was the relationship between Rachel, Hannah and Alexa. Each time he was apprehensive towards her and her attitude with the children he would spend a weekend observing and watching. She never put a foot wrong as far as the two girls were concerned. With him it was a different matter. He could see Rachel was a good mother but a lousy wife.

Glenn devoted more and more time to his work. He also shared an enjoyment of playing golf, generally with colleagues, but this activity ran into serious trouble with his wife.

"You go off every Saturday morning and play golf leaving me alone and ignored. How can you do this? It cannot continue. You are at work all week and you are on the golf course with your male friends every Saturday. You have no time for me. I really believe you love them more than me."

"That is ridiculous Rachel. We are out or entertaining at home at least three nights during the week and every Friday and Saturday night as well. I am with you at every event we go to or dinner we give at home. A few hours playing golf two or three times a month is not unreasonable, and besides I need the activity and company of my men friends."

"You go to the gym before you come home so don't talk to me about activity." She yelled and a full-on fight followed. It was the same every time he was going out to play golf. Neither party was willing to give in.

One Sunday after lunch Glenn went up to his daughter's bedroom. It was a large L shaped room allowing each girl a little privacy yet companionship at the same time. Alexa was too small to be in a bedroom alone so it provided an excellent temporary solution. Hannah and her father were joking and laughing together when Rachel stormed in shouting and trembling with uncontrolled anger.

"What do you two think you are doing? Stop this nonsense at once. Hannah, you know this is rest time...behave yourself. Stop fooling around immediately. I will not tolerate this behaviour." Glenn looked at Hannah startled. There was absolute terror in her eyes. He then looked up at his wife. She ran downstairs screaming and crying. He now knew how serious the problem was. He pacified his daughter and then ran down the stairs after Rachel, taking her into his arms and saying.

"Rachel, that was uncalled for. I was just playing with Hannah and have every right to do so." The mother burst into hysterical tears sobbing her heart out.

"You don't love me anymore. You love Hannah more than me."

"That is ridiculous and you know it. I was only having a little fun time before they have their rest."

It was an event that Glenn would never forget. He now was convinced it was absolutely vital that he faced his wife's need for excessive admiration and never ending praise to avoid the incredible insecurity and low self-worth she constantly battled with. He saw that her fragility made her highly reactive to criticism with bouts of anger and rage. It was an intolerable situation for him to be in but he resolved to do all he could to protect his children. He at last understood her craving for attention, her outspoken, arrogant and self-loving ways and belief of her entitlement in life. He was also aware of how superficially charming she was and vowed never to give in to it again.

"I initially lived in a fairy tale before we were married. I was manipulated without seeing or understanding it and here I am dealing with a depressive individual, sheltering my two children from her nasty outbursts of rage and hostility," he said talking out loud to himself as he paced up and down. "It is only a matter of time before that hostility turns into hatred. It must be avoided."

The next few months were relatively loving and enjoyable. Nevertheless, Glenn kept a close watch on his volatile wife and as the months went by all seemed to be good. He allowed himself to relax. At long last the future again looked promising. He did notice a rather arrogant and haughty manner at certain times but accepted this as Rachel being herself. He knew she had an inflated ego from way back but had never regarded this as a threat to their relationship and subsequent marriage. He accepted that being married to an individual like his wife, an inherent low-key psychopath, meant much manipulation, but his confidence grew. Times were back to normal. He even dared playing one or two rounds of golf! His confidence was short lived.

It was Christmas day and he and Rachel were giving a Christmas Lunch for family and a few close friends. It was a happy occasion. Out of the blue one of his wife's great friends sidled up to him.

"Glenn what have I done? I am being given the cold shoulder by your wife. She will not talk to me and I have absolutely no idea what possibly the cause could be. You know about my incredible friendship with her so please tell me what is going on."

"June, I have no idea. She has not been well lately so perhaps she is fighting a little depression. Let me speak to her."

"Please do not say I mentioned anything to you...I must go," she said glancing over her shoulder. She had seen Rachel marching towards us and quickly left. June was the wife of Adrian, a good friend and business associate. Glenn naturally immediately tackled Rachel. She, however, simply shrugged her shoulders and without a word walked away. He decided not to interfere further.

A month later a similar situation arose. Glenn was mortified. His wife said nothing. Similar situations became a regular occurrence, leaving her husband bewildered and somewhat betrayed. Ideas of how difficult marriage really was and how near impossible it was to sustain and survive the long road ahead, swamped his mind and all his thoughts. He had to do something.

"Rachel, I do not understand what is going on with you and quite frankly I am close to closing shop." She panicked and tears flowed.

"Glenn I can no longer live in this place. I cannot deal with the people in this city and if our marriage is to survive we have to move." He was flabbergasted. "This place is pure hell for me. I love our holidays at Umhlanga and loved the last one in Umdloti. I want to live there and you can come for weekends to be with me and the children." He was initially appalled but slowly recognised that maybe this could work for a limited time. He phoned the Umdloti owner, took a six month lease on the property with an option to purchase and they moved down to KwaZuluNatal. He had decided to give it a try, changed his job and bought new furniture for their beach house. Glenn did not tell his father. In addition to what was essentially Rachel's move to the coast, he took the opportunity to start his own business operating out of Johannesburg.

The first month was glorious and the couple talked and planned for another baby. This time Glenn was determined it would be a boy and they both investigated exactly as to what was needed in achieving this. It was soon announced that a baby was on the way. The future looked amazingly good.

The new routine was at first both relaxing and fun. He travelled to the coast each weekend and had a marvellous two days rest. Glenn began to seriously love his increased freedom and slowly it became every two weeks with guests being invited to join them. Rachel started to occasionally feel ill apparently on account of the impending birth and Umdloti began to lose some of its appeal for them both.

Back in Johannesburg the young husband went off on a tangent and looked around for a new Johannesburg house quickly finding one in the suburb of Hyde Park, a house he considered to be the perfect home. It was large, (approximately 700 sq. metres), under thatch with two acres of ground and he immediately bought it. Bit by bit they made their way back to Johannesburg, eventually selling their current Illovo home and prepared to move into the new house. Glenn had felt that the marriage was failing mainly due to the less loving and nurturing of each other. He controlled himself, but they both felt a diminishing empathy existing between each other which naturally resulted in some cruel behaviour. Nasty outbursts of rage took control of Rachel. She suspected she had lost her victim and had no power over him. She refused point blank to allow Glenn take Fred, the family dog, to the new home and threatened not to move in if he insisted the dog remained. He had to give in but would never forgive her or forget this. He knew they had to stay together for the children's school years but vowed to leave her as soon as the not yet born son left school. Alterations to the new home were completed and they moved in. Glenn and Rachel simply tolerated each other. The girls loved the rambling new house. Their father told them it was their forever home. He also took his parents to see it.

"It is glorious Glenn and I wish you many years of happiness. Strangely enough I know the house. You, without realising it, purchased it from a South African co-director of mine. I believe he has built a new home further down in the cul-de-sac. Quite a coincidence don't you think?"

"Yes, Rachel met with the wife but unfortunately was rather rude to her. I spoke to Rachel about how she treated some people but as per usual she got defensive saying something about not wanting to speak to neighbours. Dad, I cannot carry on living like this. Everything she does is self serving although to people in general she is considered appealing and, her overbearing enthusiasm, amusing. Some people are naturally drawn to her albeit in small doses and find her attractive, charismatic and exciting. She obviously takes advantage of these situations and thrives on being the centre of attraction, loves talking about herself and uses this to exaggerate anything she has or intends to accomplish. All I do is look on."

"My son, the time has come for you to call in professional help, not for her but for you. See where that takes you. In my opinion this is a basic necessity if you are to understand what you have got yourself into and how to deal with it. I cannot get involved here myself and have no intention of giving you any advice. You need a professional to do that."

Glenn agreed and subsequently went to see someone he casually knew, stipulating that on no account were the children or their mother to be approached. He felt confident that a solution would be found.

"Hello Glenn, nice to see you and I hope I can give you the advice you are looking for."

"Good to see you too, Doctor. What I would like to do is give you an outline of my problem and possibly you can help me with the way forward. I feel my main difficulty is the little understanding I have or, more directly put, the lack of understanding I have, of what is going on in my life and more importantly how I should deal with it. I am talking about a troubled wife and two young children with a third on the way."

Glenn proceeded to give him an outline since his marriage and the reactions from both Rachel and him of life in general.

"I understand your predicament my friend but to be honest I really need to talk to Rachel if we are to move forward. There is absolutely no doubt that she is a troubled lady trapped in a very complex situation, a situation created by both of you. Would you mind if I spoke to her, confidentially of course?"

"I am really not keen on that. I feel it is too early. Perhaps, we should leave it for the moment and when I get the opportunity to broach the subject, I will suggest it, but be warned, she is an extremely complicated person and is highly unlikely to want to talk to you."

"Very well, we will see how things progress, but I am convinced the only way to tackle the problem is dialogue. There is a strong possibility, from what you have told me, that Rachel has psychopathic tendencies. I gather this from your fairy tale relationship and subsequent marriage but that is where a nightmare can unfold. Dating and marrying a psychopath involves being subjected to a lot of manipulation and there is no doubt from what you say that you have been constantly manipulated. Just remember, nothing is out of the question once a psychopath has lost control of their victim. Horrific outbursts of rage, combined with all round hostility, surfaces when there is any hint or suspicion of rejection. They set out to destroy relationships with friends, (mutual or otherwise) and, of course, use the children to achieve their goals. I am not saying your wife is a psychopath but from what you say, there is a possibility in the affirmative. You must be on the watch constantly."

Glenn left a little shocked and continued with his life as before.

A few months later a disaster occurred that was instrumental in changing his life. His wife Rachel killed their unborn son. She was in her seventh month of pregnancy meaning her unborn baby was capable of being born alive.

It started off as a typical weekday. Glenn had taken the girls to Kingsmead as Rachel claimed she had a hairdresser's appointment plus one or two other things to do. He also agreed to collect them. He was a little surprised by her request as she was the one who always insisted it was her duty to take and fetch their daughters to and from school. Not expecting anything untoward, he agreed. He proceeded to carry out his duties and on returning to the house was rather surprised to note his wife was not back nor had she contacted him. He thought nothing more of it. She returned home shortly before 3pm. looking a little agitated but reasonably normal. Thirty minutes later she announced she had 'lost the baby'.

"What do you mean you have lost the baby?" he asked in a controlled but brittle voice.

"I got rid of it. I do not want it," she grunted. "I have two girls and that is enough. I cannot talk about it," she growled going into the bedroom.

Glenn could get nothing more out of her. He began to panic and immediately phoned their gynaecologist but, alas, the doctor claimed the entire event was covered by Doctor/Client confidentiality and that only she could tell what had happened. Glenn then again insisted he needed to know. The doctor would not budge.

"Glenn, I am unable to say anything further," and he disconnected the call. He had sounded agitated and concerned. Glenn marched into their bedroom battling to control his anger and emotions.

"Please explain to me what is going on," he pleaded as gently as possible.

"Face the fact the baby has gone. It is over and I am so pleased to tell you this. Now leave me alone."

"You have killed our son and I have no alternative but to take this matter to the police."

"Do what you like. I could not care what you do but remember you will only destroy your darling daughters, and that means your beloved Hannah. Now leave me alone!" Glenn jumped into his car and charged off to the Parkview Police Station and sat outside their offices for well over an hour pondering all avenues open to him. He squirmed and writhed in agony feeling absolutely helpless and totally miserable. He subsequently drove home defeated. He knew Rachel had lost all control of reality and had definitely lost control of him, her victim. It was the end of Rachel for Glenn Edward Kirk.

The following months were completely sterile of any affection or love between the two. Rachel remained very mentally fragile and thus highly reactive to criticism of any sort. She remained outspoken, arrogant, self-loving and continued to have feelings of ever increasing superiority which she believed gave her the right to belittle others and focus on their flaws. She also carried on working hard on exaggerating her accomplishments and the idealised image she had of herself, together with her efforts and diminishing ability to put down others. Eventually it was to no avail. The marriage meant nothing to Glenn. He wanted out. Rachel began to dream of a dark and handsome knight in shining armour whisking her away on horseback into the distant mountains. The two of them called in to see Sir Frederick and to invite comment. He was shocked beyond belief.

"This is absolutely ridiculous," he wailed, "most of Johannesburg sleeps in different bedrooms and you can do the same. Divorce is out of the question." Glenn wondered at his reaction. Lady Mary had died a few years earlier and he had remarried. Did they sleep in separate bedrooms? His son in law knew for a fact that Sir Frederick shared a suite of one main bedroom plus a very large so called dressing room that housed a very comfortable bed. Glenn had never asked any questions about this. The two left without accomplishing anything.

Glenn reluctantly accepted the decision and began to lead his own life. He played golf, generally on alternate Saturdays and started a new pastime with his St. John's colleague and business friend Derek. He joined Derek's hunting group. Rachel was furious. She still wanted to control the man she had married but she need not have worried. He was rapidly becoming his own man and would not budge. Every other weekend he was out shooting, as always, for the pot. One such weekend a disaster happened. He aimed at an impala, bringing him down with a clean shot and, as he ran up to the gentle and beautiful animal, it involuntarily raised its head, looked into his eyes, and fell back dead. Glenn was horrified and a spiritual mess. He never ever hunted again. It was this event that later led him into becoming recognised as an active but silent world wildlife conservationist and an avid animal activist.

The marriage continued but not without numerous attacks from Rachel. It was all part of her aim to destroy his relationships with friends and more particularly their two children. Suddenly, out of the blue, a decision was made, by her, that the children were to leave Kingsmead immediately and go to the local primary school of the area. Her reason for this was the claim that Rosebank Primary offered a superior education at a much lower monthly levy. He fought tooth and nail with her over this and saw it as a direct attack on him. He had on many occasions voiced to friends how extremely satisfied they were with what Kingsmead had to offer. Furthermore, his father had recently announced he would in future be responsible for all Kingsmead costs for his two grandchildren. No amount of urging would change Rachel's mind and so the girls moved. No doubt she would later regret this but Glenn was nevertheless mortified.

Then something happened that changed everything. Rachel announced she had consulted with a member of her family, a lawyer, and divorce proceedings were in progress. In addition to this, her father had given consent to the divorce. Glenn was astounded but incredibly thankful. It was agreed he would keep the house, (his father had provided some of the finance towards its purchase), and she would take a small flat at the bottom of Central Avenue in Athol. A monthly payment to her was approved by both parties and the children would live with their mother. Alternate weekends were spent with each parent. He later discovered Rachel had announced that, he, Glenn preferred the company of men to being with her. He never bothered to reply. At last she was out of his life. His interest remained principally for his children and an active lifestyle. Women, and essentially marriage, were out of consideration for the time being and the future looked uncluttered and promising. Unfortunately for Glenn that was not the case.

CHAPTER 7.

The first few months of his newly divorced life were enjoyable and the future seemed good. Glenn was in the midst of a new business enterprise and travelled widely in Africa, England and Europe, particularly Holland. There were hiccups when dealing with the African side of things particularly where imports to those countries were concerned. Malawi and Zambia posed continuing problems but he managed matters well and could see a promising future ahead. He, however, relied heavily on his South African attorney and personal friend, Mervyn, to help sort out discrepancies and make necessary adjustments but what he did not foresee was the continual difficulties surrounding his ex-wife and children. The two girls had been bitterly upset by the divorce and it was evident that some internal stirring was being done on another level. In addition to this, the alternate weekend visitation rights worked but the goodbyes were another matter. Then, there was the school choice problem. No matter how hard he tried to accept the Rosebank Primary School situation he genuinely felt the move had been an appalling mistake forced through by his ex-wife. The situation was becoming intolerable. In addition to this it was discovered his special love, Hannah, was dyslexic. He had always thought Rachel could be dyslexic on account of her inability to spell or construct reasonable sentences. Her family had treated it as an amusing joke, but it had never occurred to him it would filter down to his darling daughter. Kingsmead had somehow helped her but the new school had no facilities and no interest. What was he to do?

Suddenly everything took a dive downwards. A mutual friend came to see Glenn and announced that Rachel was planning to live in England and was talking of taking the children out of the country.

"Dad, what am I to do?" asked Glenn of his father.

"My boy, first think of our financial presence in the United Kingdom. Our assets are in what I call self-propagating investments but the time will come when you may want to take a direct part in their control and administration. In fact, I am hoping that will be the case. I am not going to be here for ever and the loss of your son Sebastian has been a tragic reality which means you really have no choice but to handle everything yourself. Hannah and Alexa clearly have no investment acumen or ability, well not at this stage anyway, so it is all over to you for now and, indeed for the future as I see it. Let things continue as they are and wait for Rachel to tell you what her plans are. It was our intention to send the girls to school in England. By the way, I personally see a plummeting rand and an impossible situation for your ex-wife."

Seven days later another mutual friend also told Glenn about the impending move. He consulted his attorney.

"Mervyn, the mother of my children is a nut case. How can I allow them to be at her beck and call in the United Kingdom? What worries me most is the hate and deceit she has in her plus the damage she will do trying to destroy any feelings they have for me. It is an impossible situation."

"Glenn, what is a typical Sunday for you and your daughters? I know you don't cook so do you ever take them out?"

"Yes, I do. We often go to the Inanda Club for lunch. It is actually one of their special weekend treats."

"Perfect, give a luncheon there this coming weekend. I will be present with a local leading Psychiatrist who can watch the girls and assess the situation and give you a suitable report. He will tell you everything you want to know"

"That sounds good to me. I will abide by his findings. The one thing about Rachel is that she is a good mother and, if he confirms it, I will not stop them leaving the country but, I need to know what her intentions are before I take a decision."

"Good, what time will you expect us?"

"We can meet at the club at 12.30pm?"

The lunch was a great success and Hannah and Alexa were declared fun and well adjusted children.

"Glenn, your children are truly charming and appear to be well adjusted young ladies. I believe that you have no alternative but to let them go to England and, I say this, taking into account your ex-wife's problems. I hope for you and your children's sake I am wrong but quite frankly the road ahead could be tricky as far as you are concerned. From what you tell me, and that means she has not turned to anybody for mental assessment. Yes, you can expect a challenging and bumpy road ahead."

One month later Rachel brought her man George, an accountant, to see Glenn at his house in Johannesburg and announced she was going to marry him in London. Glenn breathed a sigh of relief. He also noted that this George chap was considerably older than Rachel which had to be a plus. Maybe things would be better for all concerned. George then suddenly announced that any money paid towards the children's upkeep had to be paid into an account in Switzerland which he would open expressly for this purpose. Glenn refused point blank. He also explained the constraints of the legal divorce orders and referred him to the currency exchange rate. He could see this new man was shocked even though he remained silent. Glenn also added that he would not be challenging his children leaving the country and the two of them left. He never saw him ever again.

The next year and a half was demanding as expected but the girls came to South Africa on alternate holidays and their father visited them in London whenever he could. Suddenly, out of the blue, the Kirk household was confronted with a very disturbing event. All overseas mail was arriving opened. There was no attempt to disguise this and each envelope was resealed by a printed label advising the recipient that the post had been opened as per government instructions. Each letter was clearly marked and stamped. No effort had been made to hide the fact. There was no doubt who was behind this. Glenn and his father jumped on to the next British Airways plane to London, quietly attended to the family off shore investments and were back in Johannesburg six days later, exhausted but satisfied that vulnerability was not a factor. The mounting difficulties did not end there. Hannah and Alexa spoke to their father.

"Daddy, we have something we would like to discuss with you."

"You can do so with pleasure. I am all ears!"

"Mummy said you would understand. We truly love coming to South Africa to see you for at least two of our school holidays every year but to be honest we really miss our school friends. Could we stay in London for these holidays and maybe we can be together more often there?"

Glenn was 'bowled over and out'. He was taken by complete surprise. This was not a situation he had considered or even envisaged. He gathered his thoughts and said.

"I fully understand and I will make every attempt to be in London more often. Don't worry about it girls. Friends are important."

"We knew you would understand. Mummy said you would," and that was the end of it. Glenn knew exactly where it had come from.

The next school holiday Glenn collected his daughters and they spent three days in London together and the rest of the time in the United States. It was a glorious holiday with Disney World in Florida and other attractions. It was a holiday always to be remembered. Some months later Albert Edward Kirk, a devout and well recognised freemason of The United Grand Lodge of England, (the oldest Grande Lodge in the world) and an enthusiastic entrepreneur died from an aneurysm. Glenn was devastated. He had recently moved to Cape Town but stayed with his mother in Johannesburg for a few weeks to sort out the South African assets and finances before flying off to London. His father had left a South African Will making Glenn the main beneficiary subject to a usufruct to be held by his mother during her lifetime. He had to attend to the family finances in the United Kingdom. He first called in to see Mr. Gudgin, the Manager at the National Westminster Bank and a business friend of his late father.

"I am dreadfully sorry to hear of your tragic loss Glenn. I have heard from your mother, and she has asked me to transfer money to a third party here in London. Obviously, she is, like you, a signatory to these funds and I had no trouble taking instructions from her. I was pleased to be able to help her. I also have an envelope in a private safety deposit box strictly to be opened by you only. I will fetch it."

Ten minutes later he returned with the envelope. Glenn opened it and quietly put it back into his pocket, bade Mr. Gudgin goodbye and went straight to a bank in the City of London as per the envelope's contents. He had been expected. All assets were accounted for and handed over to the relevant authorities to be registered as per Glenn's instructions. Included in this very large portfolio were 368 gold mint Kruger Coins. Much of the scrip was in bearer format or registered in a holding company's name. He recalled his father asking him to sign a second power of attorney at the same time as the first and had immediately signed and given it back to his him. Glenn left it all as it was and returned to his hotel only later going to see his beloved daughters. As always he was never invited into the house so waited outside to collect them with the three of them ending up at the local Wimpy, a favourite spot of the two girls.

"How is everything going for you two, especially at school, and what news have you got for me?"

"Daddy, I am still having trouble with reading and I am teased by the girls. They all call me posh. I miss you so much."

"I miss you too Hannah. Don't worry about the other girls. They are simply eaten up with jealousy. And you Alexa, how are you?"

She looked at her father and said, "I am fine, you must see our new room, it is beautiful. I like being a Bishop, it suits me." Glenn looked at her mortified as good old Hannah reprimanded her sister, declaring, "you are a Kirk and will always be."

Glenn had had enough and took them back to their mother's house. He was not allowed to see the bedroom as it was 'inconvenient'. Two days later he stopped off in Zurich for twenty four hours following which he returned to South Africa.

It was later when Hannah came out to South Africa principally to see friends that she surreptitiously visited Syfrets for details on her Grandfather's South African will. She was advised she was not a beneficiary and therefore not in any way part of the will. Glenn said nothing to anyone about the enquiry. He now knew Rachel had the girls well and truly under her control. A few months later Mr. Gudgin phoned him.

"Glenn, I have Rachel in my office, I am talking to you from an adjacent room in the bank. Your ex-wife is here and demanding details on all your accounts. I have explained to her that she is not part of your banking anymore, her signature was withdrawn, but I must warn you there is one safety deposit box which you forgot to include in the removal of her signature and thus, by right, I have to hand over the contents to her. I simply want you to know the circumstances I find myself in."

"Mr. Gudgin, that's odd. Can you tell me what the contents are?"

"Yes, indeed, it holds very little probably that is why it was ignored. There are 8 Kruger Rands, a share certificate, some cash and a few other items. Nothing of consequence really."

"That is quite in order. Just give it all to her." The phone was disconnected with the whole matter resolved. The next day he once again flew to London but, on this occasion, he meticulously began with the moving of all the Kirk assets to North America. It was an eighteen month exercise. He was determined not to have financial complications with his children and ex-wife ever again.

Glenn had been considering various investment strategies for some time but was hesitant as to exactly what the initial steps would be. He felt it was imperative that the entire operation would follow a legal format and be carried out within the United States legal requirements and justice system. Furthermore, everything would be done as his father had instructed which was total anonymity. Young Glenn's original first job with the mining house had been a short stint with the Merchant Banking arm, Union Acceptances, but this subsidiary had been sold a few months after him joining and he was subsequently transferred to the holding company's Head Office. Although his tenure ship was brief he was eternally grateful for the banking experience. There were numerous trips between South Africa, London and New York and, once all the Kirk assets were safely in The United States, Glenn set about interviewing what he regarded as the top three American Merchant Banks. He had various ideas about the administration and handling of Investment Portfolios but wanted a fully comprehensive investment strategy proposal of what each had in mind. He was aware that each bank required a new client to invest a substantial sum of money before they would open an investment account for him but at no stage did he intend to mention the Kirk total asset value.

It was time to meet with the merchant bank fraternity. He decided he was ready to interview three of the most relevant Banks starting with Goldman Sachs, one of the leading banking firms providing financial services to Government, Corporate, Retail and Investment Clients. He then approached Morgan Stanley and then finally Merrill Lynch (Bank of America).

 He explained to each one what he was looking for.

Consulting services through their private wealth management and private client services.

Investment in companies that exhibit strong balance sheets, solid fundamentals and most importantly have great growth potential.

He had the same reply to all proposals.

"Gentlemen, I understand where you are coming from and what you offer. I will be totally open with you. I am close to appointing an Investment Banking Enterprise to handle my affairs. I am now aware of your conditions and proposals and will consider all my options as to what you offer and will get back to you within a month or perhaps a little earlier. I have some matters to sort out over the next few weeks and once I have attended to that I will give you my undivided attention. I will remind you I hold well over 50% of my assets in cash so you will appreciate the enormity of the task that I am dealing with. Thank you for your time."

Glenn accepted that each proposal made good business sense, but he was looking for something else, something more flexible, a portfolio that represented more of what he personally wanted to see and achieve going forward. He simply had not found a direction he wanted to follow. He also knew he wanted to maintain considerable control of the investment strategies.

One evening, probably a week after his merchant bank interviews, he attended a drinks party in Upper East Side. He was not particularly fond of cocktail entertainment and most certainly not a keen drinker but realised he had a need to expand his social circle and so made the effort to attend. It was an evening that was to change his life.

"Glenn, may I introduce you to Chad and Hank," his hostess said looking towards two relative youngsters standing nearby. "Hank's wife is out of town and the two of them look a bit uncomfortable. You might enjoy meeting them as I know the three of you have some common interests." She took him over, made the required introductions and, typically of a good hostess, moved on. Pleasantries between the three men were passed and then little was said.

"What do you do in New York Glenn? I ask because of your accent and guess you are English."

"Yes I am, but with strong South African roots! I was at school there and part of my University and married life was spent in Johannesburg. I am only here for another week but will be back relatively soon. Having a bit of trouble organising business matters. And you, what do you do?"

"Both Hank and I worked for Credit Suisse here in New York, but we recently decided to go on our own. We have been friends for years, since school in fact, and now are in the investment field on our own joint account."

"Strangely enough, I am rather interested in the investment world myself. I have been talking to Goldman Sachs and a couple of other institutions but I don't seem to have a fit."

"Yip, they are a little reticent to take on new people."

"Hank, I am not interested in working for them, I am sort of interested in letting them handle a portfolio," replied Glenn.

Chad hurriedly said, "I am so sorry we just presumed you were looking for something in Management."

"Not at all." With that he walked away leaving the two Americans a little unsure of what had just happened. Chad and Hank were at least ten years younger than he was and he had actually felt no further comment was necessary. Glenn noticed they watched him talking to a few other guests but avoided talking to them further and was about to bid his hostess goodbye when he found Chad once again at his side.

"Glenn, so sorry about earlier. What about lunch on Thursday?" The three of them agreed to meet and promptly left.

Thursday lunch was at a bistro type restaurant in East Village and was a perfect backdrop for good, relaxed conversation and favourable talks. Glenn had agreed to the meet up on a casual friendship basis not expecting anything more.

"Well Hank, Chad, what do you two actually do? Perhaps I should start with my background. I am a visitor but will probably be spending much of my time here in New York. My interest actually has something to do with the financial markets which I am only watching from the side lines at present. I have had a few portfolio suggestions put to me but nothing has suited as to what I want. Now over to you, where does your financial expertise lie?"

"Glenn, we recently formed our own financial planning enterprise. As you know, Chad and I previously both worked for Credit Suisse as Investment Advisers and have recently opened up our own Financial Services Company. We are registered and licensed as a receiver of deposits and other financial services such as wealth management, so it is a bona fide consultant enterprise. Confidentially, we have stepped out of our previous jobs together with three clients who, I must emphasise, remain as clients and not shareholders which leads me to the next important factor. We are constantly looking for new business."

"Thank you for getting to the point so quickly. My reply is that I am interested in seeing what you can offer me. I just want you to know a fairly large sum of money is involved and I will be slowly, or perhaps better described as gently, moving forward. Hopefully we can find some sort of future together. I will be away for a month and as soon as I get back, we can take this further. What do you say Gentleman?"

"Sounds good to me."

"And to me," joined in Chad. The remainder of the lunch was relaxed with all three in excellent humour.

CHAPTER 8.

Glenn sat back in his Cape Town study feeling concerned about liquidating the last of his local assets when his thoughts turned to his daughters. He had never recovered from the devastating loss of his unborn son whom he called Sebastian and had accepted, to a degree, the growing chasm between himself and his two remaining children, Hannah and Alexa. Possibly once he was more settled in New York he might find a way to resolve the situation equably for all concerned but he harboured growing doubts. He thought of the numerous problems encountered in his married life and accepted his indifference to the collapse of the marriage. The reality was his life had improved beyond measure in recent years but there was the niggling doubt he could have done more to help Rachel with her increasing mental problems. He phoned his Johannesburg Doctor, Martin Lawrence.

"Good morning doctor, do you remember me."

"Indeed, I do Glenn. How are you keeping and more importantly, how are your daughters handling living in the U.K.?"

"It is good to hear your voice! Things have improved somewhat but do you have a few minutes to spare?"

"Most certainly." The same old Dr. Lawrence thought Glenn.

"I am in Cape Town and want to quickly go through the problems I had with my ex-wife Rachel. I have this nagging doubt that I did not do enough to help her. The marriage was doomed shortly after Hannah's birth, that I know, and I am thankful to be out of it. My reason for thinking of her and her behaviour is my children and the situation they and I find ourselves in. It is an ongoing matter over which I seem to have no control."

"Stop right there Glenn. You must understand all the implications of what you are dealing with right from the word go. It is not for me to go into her personality disfunction, but I believe your problems really began when her mother died. There are many family disorders, including bad marriages plus multiple deaths that surround families. Your father-in-law was part of this and I suspect your troubles seriously took hold due to his behaviour after his first wife died and I am including in this his self-officiating early morning phone calls plus the many other additional calls he made to Rachel. I am not going to go into this in detail, but I urge you to consider it. I would like to point out the chief characteristics of a psychopath and ask you to try and apply them to your situation. Maybe you will find similarities with your ex-wife and even see if her father also had similar issues. It can often be a genetic issue passed down from parent to child. Hopefully you will then be able find a little solitude.

Firstly, and foremost, psychopaths are likeable people with good conversational ability and often display a certain amount of charisma and humour.

They enjoy action in their lives and hence often struggle to stay engaged in particular events and routines.

They definitely have an inflated view of themselves seeing themselves as important and entitled.

They are very good at getting other people to do what they want and thus are very manipulative.

They do not worry how their behaviour affects other people and believe if they hurt a person that person is overacting and should get over it. Hence, they do not experience any guilt or pain if others are involved, and they use people to get whatever they can.

They generally exhibit behavioural problems at an early age.

They respond to things according to the way they feel and indicate indifference to promises and reality.

They may get married because it serves them well but their behaviour often leads to divorce as their partners eventually see them in a different light.

This is a brief summary of general characteristics which hopefully will help you in some way. Please remember that to be classified as a psychopath does not have to involve all these characteristics. Perhaps you might consider approaching a certified psychiatrist for guidance and counselling. If you do please don't hesitate to ask. I will consult with my colleague Findlay, but I do also know of someone in London. New York however, is another matter."

"Doctor, thank you so much. What you have outlined is very much in line with many of the problems experienced during our marriage and leaves me feeling somewhat better."

"Good Glenn, but remember, please consult with a more qualified individual should this persist. I am only a general practitioner, a family doctor."

Glenn relaxed and turned his attention to what he regarded as more important matters, America.

He had much to do in Cape Town but could not rest knowing all his affairs in New York were in a state of flux. He was the first to recognise he was not a standard type of individual that required the services of a high-end normal banking enterprise but at the same time he had to safeguard what had been achieved by him and his late father. Added to this was the emotional and unhealthy situation with his daughters. He had sent another three letters to them in London but no replies were forthcoming. He had included payments in the third and was aware the exchange rate between the South African Rand and the British Pound was rapidly deteriorating but this was a situation his ex-wife had to manage. It had been her choice to remove the children from his custody. He had been forced to take note of her mental health issues when considering the new custody arrangements and the move to the UK. Rachel would always regard her ex-husband as her number one enemy, and she would never stop trying to destroy his relationship with the two girl's and he had no doubt she would continue playing with their minds. His daughters were his priority and he followed this religiously. It was an extreme high-risk situation and had to be handled with sensitivity and compassion. This, together with the constant distressing thoughts about his late son, controlled his mind. Things were not what he wanted them to be and a month later Glenn returned to New York City. It was time to move forward with his American project. There was so much to do.

Two days after touching down on American soil Glenn contacted Chad.

"Hi Chad, any chance of the three of us getting together?"

"Most definitely Glenn, when suits you?"

"Tomorrow, we can meet at the same restaurant as before and chat over lunch. Does that suit you."

"Most definitely, see you tomorrow, 12.30pm."

In the morning Glenn was up early and ready to get going. He first had to view a small apartment which was an absolute necessity. The decision to get himself settled more permanently was a priority. He had already decided it had to be somewhere near a suitable dog Run, (a dog park), possibly in the financial district. He was totally attached to his two dogs. Glenn had been an English Springer Spaniel fan for a number of years and was in the habit of taking his dogs with him wherever he travelled, dependant of course on the time factor involved. It was not worthwhile for short international visits on account of the travelling time ratio. Comfort was a consideration for all three of the Kirk family, Glenn plus his dogs. The New York trip was particularly exhausting, both for him and them, so happiness and ease of travelling was a prime consideration. He intended to eventually follow a stay of six months at a time with an absence of a further six months which meant special dog facilities in New York was on the cards. He still had his house in Cape Town so accommodation for him and them was semi sorted in South Africa but for now investment action came first.

"You two look good," exclaimed Glenn as they sat down together. "It is good to see you again."

"For us too," retorted Chad. "We know how you like to get to the point in everything that is business and are genuinely keen to come to some arrangement as per your investment portfolio."

"Yes, I have some thoughts in mind so let me begin."

"You are both aware that I have met with three of the largest banks in the city. I have not mentioned it previously, but I qualify as an

64

investment client in each case. They are all solid enterprises with top end clients and are recognised as the finest available and I find this very comforting. You will appreciate how important this is to a relative newcomer to the American Market like myself. However, after much thought I have reached the conclusion I must follow what I believe is best for me. I would like to work with your company on a trial basis for the first six months and on my terms. We can get together after the six months are up and examine the entire mechanism and relationship between the three of us. I fully understand you both represent your company and you must appreciate that I talk on behalf of my holding company and its three subsidiary companies."

"I am sure we can work around your requirements Glenn," assured Chad, "but Hank and I will need to examine matters from our side before final acceptance. Glenn, could you explain the structure of your investments.?"

"With pleasure," replied Glenn politely. "I have a holding company which is, in essence, the heart of my overall activity. The first subsidiary is what you people call 'widow and orphan' shareholdings. I personally do not use that terminology although it is the home for my medium to long term holdings or, as you might prefer to say, blue chip investments. Whatever title you use it is self-explanatory. Conservative investment principles are the norm. The second subsidiary holds more speculative shares. I look to decent growth here, income is not a necessity. The third company is solely for venture capital investments. I alone carry responsibility for all investment decisions made and my signature is required on all policy instruction. Obviously this is reviewable as we grow and more flexibility becomes necessary. Does this give you some idea of how I operate?"

"It certainly does. The two of us will discuss our side of things which will without doubt require more clarification as we go forward. You have mentioned before that you have accounting and legal facilities available to you so presumably, we will be working closely with them?"

"Indeed, particularly with regard to legal and tax matters. I do insist on everything being totally legal," replied Glenn in his standard formal business manner. "That will be all for now Gentleman. If we do go ahead there will be a mountain of work for all of us to do. I can assure you I am a pleasant and understanding client, well, most of the time! It is my intention to meet with you in a few days should we both agree to go ahead."

The next matter on Glenn's list was permanent accommodation. He had decided on a single bedroom apartment, preferably one that had a similar but separate set up on the same floor or building. He appointed an agent and explained in some detail as to what he was looking for suggesting that the financial district might provide him with all his needs.

"The most important criteria for me is that two dogs must be allowed and anything you show me has to be near a dog friendly, open green area."

"I understand what you say but may I first show you something which is, I think, precisely what you are looking for. It meets those two requirements, well nearly, is in the Chelsea part of Manhattan and that is all I am going to say."

"I am prepared for whatever you choose to show so let us start off with Chelsea. It actually is one of my favourite areas, but I have not considered it at all. The church I belong to, St. Peter's, is in Chelsea, 346 West 20th Street. Strange as it may seem, my church in London is St. Peter's, Notting Hill and in Hermanus, St. Peter's, The Fisherman."

They arrived twenty minutes later, entered the condominium, took one look around and Glenn suddenly asked with a wide grin on his face, "what and where do I sign?". Two days later he was, subject to the final contract, the proud owner of a Manhattan home. The apartment had originally been two separate two bedroom, two bathroom units, but a previous owner had chosen to make them one. Glenn had found exactly what he was looking for and could not have been happier. He was absolutely delighted! Furthermore, it was in an ideal position for his two dogs. He had been a little disturbed by not hearing from his daughters and really needed an uplift like this for going forward.

Glenn sent Hannah a letter once a month giving general news and enclosing his monthly contribution as per the divorce agreement but had never received a reply. Rachel's husband had rather insistently demanded that the contribution must be paid to his account in Switzerland, but Glenn had very definitely decided this was not appropriate and hence sent it to his elder daughter. Nothing had ever been acknowledged. He was at a total loss as what to do.

It was now time to deal with the final blocks of his American Business Programme. He called Hank and Chad.

"Good Morning Hank, are you and Chad ready for further discussion and decision taking on my proposals?"

"We certainly are. We have a few questions and hopefully we will all be ready to agree on what the immediate action is to be. Can you make it at 2.30 this afternoon?"

"Perfect, I look forward to it."

He arrived on time, determined to get matters moving, be it with these two or someone else.

"Good Afternoon Gentlemen, I trust you have considered all proposals from both our sides so I suggest you give me a final outline of what you have in mind."

"Glenn, we are very interested in handling your financial investments. We have three existing clients and a fourth is definitely attractive and sought after by us. Investors such as you are in high demand by all private wealth managers, including us. We do however require a little additional information." Glenn said nothing. "We need an estimate value of the assets that will be under our care which will include current investments and cash held."

Glenn replied with a figure and an investment breakdown watching them carefully as he did so. He concluded and advised them he had one strictly non-negotiable proviso. Anonymity had to be observed at all times.

"Hank, Chad, I will explain further. The holding company is controlled by me in every way possible. Income from the three subsidiaries will be used at my discretion but I will say, my overall plan is for all income to be reinvested as I will not be making personal withdrawals.

I was at school in South Africa which is a country close to my heart, but I have long seen a frightening future ahead there. I travelled to South Africa for a study break during my London student days. My parents were only there for the first week, but I had assured my late father I would visit a local township and hospital in Johannesburg which I did. It was one of the most heart wrenching things I have ever had to do. During my first visit, to Alexander township, I witnessed a major health problem which was seriously affected by a massive rodent infestation. This was the norm. The young and the elderly were particularly at risk. There were many cases of baby's fingers, noses and other body parts being eaten by rats. The shockingly poor drainage, leaking sewage and rotting food meant people were never far from a rodent. A possible solution to the problem was the introduction of owls, (a favourite bird species of mine), for their rat catching prowess but the local resident's strong belief in witchcraft caused havoc amongst the owl population. The birds were viciously mutilated. They suffered decapitation, their eyes were cut out and their legs cut off. The brutality was almost beyond belief."

"Wow Glenn, I have never heard anything like this before," exclaimed Chad. "I cannot image the depth of depravity you speak of. What were the thoughts racing through your mind at the time? I am shocked to the core both by these inherited beliefs and the pain they inflicted on the incredibly beautiful owls that tried to live with them and help them."

"How did you cope with witnessing this?" gasped Hank.

"It did not stop there. There were many problems but another heartache for me was my seeing the horrific conditions of the roaming mixed breed dog population plus the effects of dog fighting imposed on many of them. Added to this was the malnutrition and general lack of care of the animals. It was difficult to witness and impossible to comprehend. I also had promised my father I would visit Baragwaneth Hospital on the outskirts of Johannesburg. He had arranged both trips. It was just as indescribably awful and upsetting to see. There I saw total misery. Some of our workers had been admitted over the weekend. They suffered stab wounds and in many cases paralysis. When I asked them how the injuries happened, (the most common injury being stabbing with sharpened bicycle wheel spokes), all they could say was, 'it was my friend who did it'. This should give you a glimpse as to why I am together with you today. I firmly believe education is paramount in Africa and, indeed, the rest of the world. My immediate priority is animal welfare and wildlife conservation." He could see they were totally shocked. He chose not to say anything more on the subject.

"Gentleman, I am happy to go forward with your proposal and suggest you draw up an agreement covering our relationship and valid for six months which will give us time to deal with matters arising during this initial period."

"Glenn, I feel everything has been covered and the six month trial period is definitely appreciated. We will have the document drawn up and ready for signature by tomorrow evening."

"Excellent," replied Glenn with finality.

He received the written agreement the next day, discussed it with his lawyer, and the three of them formally signed it the following evening. At last celebrations were in order. It was the beginning of a major relationship lasting many years.

CHAPTER 9.

Glenn had always felt a special affinity with animals especially those that relied on general household humanity to survive. He had an ardent love for all animals, particularly for dogs, but having been at boarding school followed by a few academic years in both South Arica and the United Kingdom, it had remained relatively stagnant. This had all changed during an episode while out hunting some years back and he had, then and there, quietly vowed to himself to devote part of his life to wildlife conservation. He firmly believed it was time for action.

Something he had read, years back, had always been in his mind and he was now ready to devote time and energy to a new project, animal conservation and animal welfare.

"We do not inherit land, water, and wildlife from our parents-----we borrow them for our children." (Author unknown).

He fervently believed this.

With more than one third of all wildlife species at risk to extinction mostly through habitual loss, climate change, invasive species or emerging diseases, something had to be done and, to be done fast. Mankind was generally at the root of this frightening scenario and the only way he could see a turn-around was in innovative collaborations between conservationists, landowners and all humanity in general. In believing that much of the hard work would take place behind the scenes he strongly felt that he needed, in these circumstances, to be involved in every way possible. He required no personal acknowledgement in any format for his work. Anonymity was the family password his father had taught him to use and follow.

Glenn decided to start with a visit to The World Wildlife Fund Offices in Washington where he quickly realised that the numerous employees and many sections in which they were involved was not what he was looking for. The commitment and strength of the staff he met appeared to be genuine and relentlessly committed to the organisation and it's cause but, he wanted more of a hands on approach for himself. He knew he wanted to help with the survival of nature by finding solutions that would save the incredible array of life on the planet and by doing so would also save mankind itself. Saving nature however, was, in his opinion, the very heart of conservation. He was deeply aware that the looming wildlife crises that was invading earth had to be neutralised and destroyed before it was too late and impossible to achieve. The planet had to become a happy and healthier place and the people of the world had a sacred duty to protect all animals and wildlife for future generations.

The areas of concern for him were:

1.The rampant wildlife crime found throughout the world. It had to be stopped. This was directly related to trade in illegal wildlife products.

Elephant ivory was still found in many commercial outlets where there is a steady consumer demand for all elephant body parts. This consumer demand had to be stopped. The illegal killing of elephants decimates global elephant populations and yet the trade continues to increase at an alarming rate.

2.Rhinoceros Poaching for Rhino products, principally the rhino horn, for use by the Chinese and Vietnamese as a traditional medicine, but recently heavily used as a status symbol to display success and wealth. Most of Africa's rhinos are to be found in Southern Africa, mainly Botswana, Zimbabwe, Namibia and South Africa. South Africa being the country that holds most of the world's rhinos and, it being Glenn's so-called home turf, he felt that it was there where he should investigate poaching in general and Elephant and Rhino poaching in particular.

He flew back to New York, attended to matters requiring his immediate attention and returned to South Africa. Fortunately, he had not yet sold his home in Cape Town.

We protect wildlife for many reasons but foremost for Glenn was the integral aim of keeping alive the balance of nature. He saw saving nature as being at the very heart of conservation and indeed at the very heart of the world, and firmly believed it was vital for him, and the rest of earth's population, to find solutions that save the incredible array of life on our planet. He fervently believed mankind could not afford to fail in this mission to save a living planet. He gave himself two days to settle in and then set out on a fact finding mission, spending the next few weeks meeting people and discussing conservation on all levels, hoping this would enable him to make a more informed decision on what to do and how to go about it.

Glenn soon felt he needed to personally inspect one or two poaching areas and phoned Dirk, a contact he had been given. Dirk suggested the surrounds to the Kruger National Park.

"Glenn, your timing is excellent! An anti-poaching unit has moved into the area less than two days ago. We can join them tomorrow. There is also a plan to divide the area into sections to facilitate the counting of elephant and rhino in their respective herds, but you and I will only participate in catching the poaching culprits." It was an ideal situation and suited his purpose perfectly. The two of them flew in the next morning to join the unit.

The helicopter made a loud whirring noise as it flew high enough to see the surrounding plains below and the herds of wildlife darting away at different angles from the flight path. It was an enthralling experience for Glenn and brought home the majesty and beauty that was Africa but also the vulnerability of the world's animal kingdom.

Glenn and his group landed and settled in for the night. In the early hours of the morning they set off following the adjacent river bed. Soon the evidence of poachers seemed to be all around them together with many snares and carcasses. It was horrifying. Glenn was totally distraught. He understood the deathly game poachers played but he had never for one moment fully understood the dire destruction and cruelty they created. Their pure evil was evident everywhere. That night he lay awake for many hours trying to formulate some sort of message to the world that life on this planet of ours had to be afforded utmost respect on all levels to ensure the prospect of health and longevity. All animals deserved this. We all deserved it.

The next day the group crossed the river keeping a constant guard against crocodiles and any possible encounters with hippos. They followed the river's pathway where it was more likely to find snares to disentangle and hopefully any poacher's overnight camps. They suddenly turned inwards towards the grassland and into the wind. The increasing smell of death came upon their group and suddenly the stench of death surrounded them. They had stumbled on a scene of demented horror, rampant death and vile destruction. Three rhino horns had been hacked from their still warm bodies, blood still trickling from their ripped flesh and gunshot wounds. A noise was heard from nearby bushes. They quickly surrounded the small outcrop, and, without further warning, two young baby rhinos stood before them with absolute terror in their eyes, both covered in the blood of their butchered mothers. The accompanying wardens jumped into action calling for urgent assistance. These little ones needed immediate attention if they were to survive.

"This is a war zone," Glenn cried as he tried to help. "May the perpetrators rot in hell."

He looked from left to right, appalled by what he saw and battling to stomach the horrific scene in which he found himself.

"I don't think I can handle this. Dirk, I must leave this side of conservation to you. The way forward is to obliterate all poachers and their syndicates throughout the world. It can be done but only by highly efficient and organised forces backed by a strong and legitimate legal system. My responsibility will have to be a financial one."

"Mr Glenn, these days poachers are being supplied by international crime gangs with seriously sophisticated equipment to track and kill rhinos. Often it is a tranquiliser gun that brings down the animal and the horn is hacked off leaving the rhino to wake up in excruciating pain and bleeding to death. These poachers are frequently also armed with rifles and hand guns and are themselves deadly death machines with absolutely no regard for what they destroy. Yes, they are evil personified."

Glenn could take no more. He left and made his way back to Cape Town. So much needed to be done but where to start was all he could think about.

He generally had an ordered mind and tried to work out some sort of purpose and action that would help him achieve his goal towards animal welfare and stop extinction of any form. He needed to put pen to paper.

Saving nature is at the very heart of conservation.

Humans are behind the current rate of species' extinction. There had been a 50% decline in animal populations in the last thirty years.

Solutions needed to be found that save the extraordinary array of life on our planet.

The decline of mammals, birds, fish, reptiles and amphibians was accelerating. This included the cultural loss of iconic species like tigers, rhinos, elephants and whales.

Reading this a few times, he was again faced with the reality that mankind cannot fail in the mission to take care of and save the living planet it inhabited. He asked himself.

"What are the principal reasons we need to do this." He knew the answers.

Nature nurtures a sense of wonder and is an integral part of survival.

He then continued writing.

What are the solutions?

Wildlife crime around the world is rampant and has to be stopped.

Drones and infra-red cameras that can detect poachers in the dead of night?

Combat trade in illegal wildlife products.

Elephant ivory is still found throughout the world. Illegal killing of elephants decimates global populations. They are killed for their tusks and find a ready market in China and Vietnam and with travellers worldwide.

Fishing feeds billions of people and is vital to economies of countless people, but unsustainable practices litter the ocean with deadly traps and mountains of plastic killing marine mammals, turtles and seabirds.

Glenn put down his pen and thought long and hard. He couldn't save the world! He decided to investigate the latest abilities of drones and what other measures were used to counter poaching. Drones had been in use from the early 1940's but their further development was something he knew little about. He also decided to examine deforestation around the world and its effect on clean air, water, food and products. He firmly believed that natural resources were vital to all living life, and had to be looked after, improved and updated wherever necessary.

He picked up the phone and talked further with Dirk.

"Dirk, my friend, if I may call you that, what do you feel is the most effective way of stopping active poaching?"

"Hello Glenn, I think one has to have direct protection work such as training and equipping rangers, community scouts and eco-guards to monitor and protect elephant and rhino populations. Added to this are dog-handler units for the actual tracking of the would be poachers. I have also thought about your suggestion of all round education and can see how very important this actually is. I also like your suggestion that local governments must come forward and join the process, manage protected areas, and assist with a regular census of the wildlife itself. This would be an enormous help."

"Dirk, I appreciate what you have to say and have noted it accordingly. It appears we have many similar ideas and concepts about the way forward. I see poaching and wildlife crime as a huge illicit international business in the same light as dangerous gangsters operating worldwide in illegal drugs and differing weapon syndicates. In my opinion there is no difference whatsoever. These businesses go side by side with weak governance and rampant corruption. Enough said."

"I am so grateful for your insight and interest and cannot wait to hear of what your next steps will be. Glenn, please don't forget us here in South Africa!"

"I certainly won't. I am only at the entry stage level so do not expect immediate dynamic action or free flowing finance, but I will keep in contact and a big thank you for allowing me to see, at first hand, how these poachers operate."

It was now clear to Glenn that illegal wildlife trade was a global challenge and that he would have to be somehow instrumental, or partly so, in creating and participating in a wildlife partnership to combat the sickening evil of poaching and trafficking that currently existed throughout the world. His financial interests had definitely taken an interesting step forward in a new and demanding global direction.

Glenn saw, what was a mish mash of small wildlife partnerships and differing efforts around the globe and believed his first step was to initiate an international cohesiveness between all people to combat poaching. This included a collaborative program facilitating connection across borders, building institutional capacity to conserve life, reduce threats, and, not to ever be forgotten, the never ending sustainable financing that would be required to keep it all afloat. It was not going to be in any way an easy task. He was totally occupied and absorbed daily in this new direction for most of the next two months and, at the end of it all, felt he had a satisfactory plan to start the process. He returned to the United States, his Springer Spaniel, as always, at his side.

"Gentleman it is good to be back and I must thank you for the feedback and initiative you have shown during my absence. I personally feel we are moving forward in the right direction. Hank, I appreciate your enthusiasm for the computer industry and your various suggestions but please remember I am part of 'The Old School' and it will take time for me to adjust. We have a venture capital vehicle for new ventures, but I do like to take new concepts slowly.

You are aware that my basic investment strategy is centred around the word 'VALUE' and you must agree we see little of that in this industry. Yes, I know future earnings must be considered but some of the figures given are created, in my view, on pure speculation and nothing else. Having said this, I am happy for entry into capital venture projects of up to a total of US$2million. Please understand this is an overall amount for the industry as a whole and not per project. We can revue, when necessary, but the due diligence approach will apply. It is very easy to let emotions take over in such situations which can end in a sector catastrophe."

"Glenn, we understand your hesitation but in our view it is a massive growth area and it would be unwise to ignore what the market feels. The figure you give is, in my opinion, ridiculously low especially when one considers our overall investment total. However, we will tread carefully."

"I leave it up to you, but you will still require my approval on each transaction. The next matter on the agenda is more of a personal one. I cannot single-handedly attend to my day-to-day diary and am looking for a personal assistant. I must emphasise this in no way concerns your affairs but if you come across a likely candidate, please let me know. Finally, I have an adjoining apartment which is my work space. Please note that all future meetings regarding matters pertaining to our business relationship will be held there."

"Glenn, we normally conduct all our meetings from our own offices and would prefer to keep it that way."

"I understand Chad, but you both need to remember we are involved in the construction of a substantial enterprise with all paperwork of each of my 4 companies held within my office. We can leave it, as is, for the moment, but I must put it on record that at some future stage it would suit me to meet and, have everything in one place."

"Very well, it is accordingly noted."

The meeting was over and Glenn left. He was paying a fair amount for their expertise and strongly felt his requirements should be recognised. There was however no need to rush things. It was not his style nor did he have any budget deadlines to meet. His wildlife's conservation direction was what troubled him and received a great deal of his attention. He saw no place for him in the large international charity organisations. He was battling with this very serious matter, his own entry into the arena, and what exactly was required to halt and dismantle the spiralling illegal operations.

A few weeks later Glenn received a call from South Africa.

"Hello Glenn, I hope I am not disturbing you or woken you for that matter."

"Hi Dirk, not at all. We are six hours behind you, time wise, so it is wake up time for New York. What can I do for you?"

"Glenn, I am in a quandary and really need some advice."

"Go ahead and talk."

"First of all, it was a tremendous pleasure to take you on that 'anti-poaching' trip and your reaction affected me deeply. Glenn, I want to take a greater part in seeing South Africa rid of the vile butchering of our wildlife. What I am saying is I want to play a greater role at grass root levels with meaningful organisation in every aspect."

"What do you exactly mean?" asked Glenn.

"I want a fully equipped unit under my control and eventually ending up with a voice to be heard at all levels as we progress."

"Dirk, I am mentally committed to conservation and have feelers out as to which way I must go. Do you have time to come to New York?"

"I can definitely make time but lack of finance is a problem. What about us meeting when you are next in Cape Town?"

"No, I will organise a return ticket and you can stay with me. If you want to do this, it must be done properly with my full support. I will get someone to contact you tomorrow, early afternoon New York time, and the two of you can arrange everything. How does that sound?"

"I cannot believe what I am hearing. I cannot wait, thank you." Dirk could hardly grasp the reality of what had just happened and immediately started preparations. Glenn at last felt he could be making headway in the throttling poaching world.

Things were looking up and then something else happened out of the blue. Glenn Geoffrey Edwards made contact! The two Glenn's met and within days G.G. (Glenn Geoffrey Edwards) found himself employed. Glenn had found his new P.A. !

G.G. was thirty years of age, had been on Wall Street for a long spell, finally left after six years and went back to surfing, his first love. He was an accomplished surfer, had enjoyed some success in the water, but after much deliberation came back to New York and asked Chad if he knew of anybody in the financial world who was looking for staff. Glenn liked his work ethics and his surfing background and employed him without a moment's hesitation.

He could not have arrived at a more suitable time. Dirk touched down at JFK Airport seven days later.

"Dirk, this is rather a momentous occasion. I am delighted to see you again and hopefully something will come of your visit for the two of us. I look forward to seeing where it takes us"

"Glenn, I feel privileged to be here. It is my first time out of South Africa, so it is, as you say, a momentous occasion!"

"How are you feeling after the long flight? A little tired I suspect?"

"Not too tired to start working," he replied laughing but Glenn could see he was exhausted.

"I will take you back to the apartment and leave you to settle in. We can have dinner together this evening and talk a little."

"That will be perfect," came his happy reply and off they went. It would prove to be the beginning of a new chapter in both their lives.

CHAPTER 10.

"Good Morning Dirk, I trust you had a good night's rest."

Dirk had in fact enjoyed a near ideal sleep and was raring to get started.

"I had a magnificent night Glenn and am ready to sit down with you whenever it suits."

"Good to hear, so tell me how you see yourself participating in South African wildlife conservation with particular reference to Rhinos and Elephants."

"Glenn, as you are aware, poaching is a wide spread issue throughout Africa and the outlook for the continent is not good. I am only equipped to talk about what goes on in South Africa.

The country has the largest populations of both Rhinos and Elephant but they are fast dwindling. All the Rhino species are currently listed as endangered and the Elephant is a close runner up on this list. Like you, I am aware CITES, (The Convention of International Trade In Endangered Species), is trying to regulate world trade but I ask you, is that enough?"

"I understand where you are coming from. In addition to what you say, Dirk, is the evidence of massive corruption, particularly on the political level, which must lead to some level of economic disintegration and will certainly place an enormous target on all animal life out there. I mention this to acknowledge what is being done, but I personally am looking at the world scenario, mainly natural resources at this stage, so have only limited time to help you in South Africa. A global partnership is what I am aiming at, coupled with wildlife conservation and crime prevention for sustainable development world-wide. Obviously, I must feel my way. I, by nature, do not rush into things so please understand that. You witnessed my deep horror at the appallingly criminal attack we came upon when we were in the African bush together, so nothing further needs to be said. I want to help you and others in South Africa but have only a limited time to do so. I will help you for an initial period of two years and we can review the situation from there. What do you say to my proposal?"

"Glenn I am honestly speechless!" Dirk replied grinning from ear to ear.

"We need to establish a groundwork, so how about over lunch? I have a newly employed assistant and would like him to join us. Give me a few minutes and I will confirm."

The three of them met up for lunch, dealt with introductions and immediately got down to business.

"Gentlemen, we are all aware of the deepening poaching crisis in South Africa. In the last fifty or sixty years around 90% of African Elephants have been wiped out either by poachers and the growing demand for ivory, changes in land use, or increasing conflict with humans. There are other reasons of which the most abhorrent for me is Big Game hunting or Trophy hunting. Rhinos are also dwindling fast as the market in rhino horn escalates daily. It is an horrific situation. Fortunately, there are people like you Dirk who are doing something about it and this is why we are sitting here today. We need to establish exactly what you need to start it happening."

"I appreciate your comments Glenn and am in your hands."

"I only want to look at basics as the beginning stage and this would first and foremost involve equipment. Dirk, you must prepare a summary of what is needed. I am not sure how we are going to handle this but obviously everything must be purchased and hence owned via a non-profit corporate set up. Similarly monthly salaries and other payments will be met accordingly. I will work on that once I have your baseline necessities. G.G., you and Dirk will liaise on this."

Glenn was just warming up. He firmly believed nothing must be left to trial and error.

"This is what I would like to do," he said turning to Dirk. "I highly recommend you go to Washington and meet members of the World Wildlife Fund. You can outline the procedures we are considering and get some feedback on their thoughts. I do not mean we take them on board. Their input, however, could be most helpful. It is a relatively short flight, a little over one hour, and I can arrange meetings with some of their most well-informed staff members who are also tackling various pressing issues with which you identify. What do you say to that?"

"That would be an enormous help Glenn."

Three days later Dirk, accompanied by G.G., flew to Washington, had meetings with three of the fund's top advisors, and returned to New York beaming broadly as they entered the condominium.

"It could not have gone better," both declared. Glenn knew they still had a mountain of work to do but said nothing. It had been a good start. Dirk went back to South Africa six days later. Glenn continued with his daily routine.

He had always enjoyed his own company and as he grew older, he allowed this characteristic to develop further in tandem with his general personality. He had from an early age built a strong protective wall around his inner being. He was definitely not a reclusive man but, probably due to his schooling and early social life, had always been hesitant to show too much affection. The experience of a disastrous marriage had steered him right back into his enjoyment of his own world, a world he shaped for himself. He had always held his emotions and feelings in check: Then he met Carol.

Carol was fifteen years younger than him, beautiful, tall, blond and excellent company. He had to admit he was mesmerised in every way possible, but he held back. Carol was an American post graduate student when the two met, strangely enough in South Africa, and they quickly found themselves enjoying each other's lives. The inevitable happened and she moved into his Cape Town house for the remaining three months of his stay. The farewell was a heart rendering 'good bye' but they both new it was for a short time only. Carol was back in the States two months later and stayed in New York before moving on to her house in Miami. The romance progressed, marriage however was never discussed. Glenn, without fully realising it, seemed to avoid the topic. Carol's manipulative powers began to show, and he inevitably and rather rapidly began to have doubts. He had from a young age attracted strong and manipulative women without him noticing it. Was he being insensitive?

"Carol, my love, I am so very involved in a relatively new wildlife project so please forgive my apparent lack of attention."

"I understand completely and have so much to sort out in Miami. I really need to be there so will leave tomorrow and you may come down as soon as you can manage it. How does that sound?" Glenn was relieved and happy with the arrangement but unfortunately for him, it was only the beginning of his troubles.

Carol phoned every evening creating an uncomfortable routine. His financial and wildlife interests came first which meant his mind was often elsewhere. How could he explain this to her? Finally, he accepted he had to be with her to talk and make her see how important his business life was to him. He firmly believed communication was the answer and she would understand.

"Yes, she will understand and realise our relationship is of importance to me," he murmured, "but also that my work is the very essence of who I am." HE phoned HER and let her know he would be in Miami the following weekend. She was totally enraptured with the news.

"Leave everything to me!" she excitingly exclaimed. "Don't worry about anything. Remember, you are leaving everything to me".

The Friday night was perfect in every way and Saturday started on the same note. It was a glorious day but Glenn felt his beloved Springer Spaniel was irritating her. Jamie loved water and was in and out of the swimming pool.

"She must learn to live with it, Jamie," he whispered to his treasured Spaniel, "don't you agree my boy?" Glenn adored his dog so that was a 'no go' situation.

"We have got sixteen people for dinner so please keep your dog out of the pool and away from our guests," she demanded. "I know it is amusing to have him sit at the table during dinner but there will not be a chair for him tonight. Glenn, love, you do need to keep better control of him when you are in the States." Glenn did not reply.

Evening came and the guests arrived. Glenn was, as is his wont at dinner parties, both charming and great company. The guests got louder as the evening progressed and he got quieter. He looked around the table studying the people and did not feel comfortable with what he saw. The majority of men wore heavy gold jewellery and were boasting about their Rolex watches, houses, yachts and cars. He stuck it out but later claimed of sinus trouble and went to bed. The next morning he told Carol exactly how he felt. She was thunderstruck. Glenn had come to realise although she was beautiful and interesting, she was not the girl for him and left for New York. Her repeated attempts to persuade him otherwise were of no consequence. He preferred his own company.

CHAPTER 11.

Glenn was becoming a little concerned. Hank and Chad had been buying into Wall Street, (all the investments had the mandatory Glenn Kirk approval) and the Venture Capital section looked top heavy. The Nasdaq index was moving upwards at what he considered to be an alarming rate which indicated remarkable investment growth on the portfolio's he had created.

"Gentleman, I am feeling a little insecure with what is happening on the market and I truly believe we are not exercising enough caution. I see record amounts of capital are flowing into Nasdaq which has to be an indication of caution being required."

"You have nothing to worry about Glenn. We must be part of the investing fraternity if we are not to be left out. An excessive cautionary approach means we will have to ignore the dot.com sector and that in turn, means us not being able to cash in on the growing use of the internet."

"I remain hesitant," replied Glenn. "There is clearly a speculative trend developing and I do not want to be part of it. I must remind you of my previous stipulation that valuations should be based on actual earnings and profits. The Nasdaq index has given a five-fold return over the last five years having risen from under 1000 to more than 5000, and quite honestly, I cannot see this continuing. A major correction is on the cards. Actual earning analysis will be the order of the day.

"Glenn we are doing precisely that."

"No, you are not from what I see before me. You are using projected earnings which is not the same thing. What worries me even more is that these projected earnings you talk about are based on guesstimates from managers and directors with little or no track record and no visible fiscal responsibility. Someone must please prepare a review of all our internet based investments. We can then meet to discuss where we go from here." Glenn could see that Hank was furious but this did not worry him. If they did not do things his way then they must move on to different pastures.

Two days later a comprehensive review was submitted. Glenn gave instructions for venture capital projects to be sold where possible and for all dot.com investments to be put on hold with the proviso of sales taking place once an informed analysis had been done. Sales had to be the order of the day.

The investment frenzy continued. The abundance of Venture Capital funding for start-ups increased and record amounts of capital flowed into the Nasdaq. Glenn's cautious approach began to worry him. Was he being unreasonably conservative? Nevertheless, he was not to be tempted and stubbornly refused to abandon his principles. He then noticed a failure of dot.com's not turning a profit. When he pointed this out to Hank, he, (Hank), simply shrug his shoulders and turned away but the truth was, he, Hank, was feeling troubled. His fear was not one of the market crashing but one of missing out on a surging Wall Street. Like many investors and venture capitalists he had abandoned a cautious approach for fear of not being able to cash in on the growing use of the internet. He, like many others, had abandoned financial wisdom and allowed himself to be swept up in the tide of 'spend …spend…spend'. Companies that still had to generate revenue and profits, (and in some cases a finished product), went to the market to see their stock prices double and triple, or more, in any one day. It was a feeding frenzy that Hank and Chad desperately wanted to be a part of. Massive amounts were paid by many, on marketing, in order to establish brands that would set them apart from the competition. Many start-ups ignored the fact they were investing as much as 90% of their budget on advertising alone as record amounts of capital flowed into the Market. Chad and Hank had joined the tide. Glenn stuck to his guns and was even ridiculed by many.

The moment of truth eventually came. The AOL Time Warner megamerger made it's appearance resulting in the biggest merger failure in history. Interest in technology companies had allowed capital to flow freely, especially to start-up companies that had no track record of success or even had a business plan or product. Suddenly a few leading high-tech companies placed large sell orders on their stocks which caused uncertainty amongst investors and within a short space of a few weeks the market crashed. The equities market tumbled from a peak 5048 in early March to 1139 in October the following year. The dot.com bubble had endured a massive burst. Dot.com Companies that had reached market capitalisations in the in the hundreds of millions of dollars became worthless in a matter of months. Many companies folded and the trillions of dollars of investment capital evaporated. Amazon, founded by Jeff Bizos in 1994, came on to the market in 1997 at US18 dollars a share, reached more than US$100 a share and had been one of Glenn's big favourites. It made its online debut in 1995 as a bookstore, which had attracted and appealed to him. It went on to add movies, music, electronics and computer software to it's diversified portfolio and as far as he was concerned Bizos could do no wrong. When the bubble burst Amazon dropped to US$10. Glenn admitted later that had been severely tempted to sell the stock held but fortunately didn't. He believed it would take, at the very least, 10 years for the market to recover.

The free-fall lasted for another two years. Glenn was relatively intact although what he considered to be internet growth stocks had left him bruised and, in one or two cases, battered. Hank and Chad lost everything. They were unemployable.

"Hank, Chad, we have been together for over ten years and I am hoping we will see at least another ten together. I am aware of your current financial situation so have an offer for each of you. You will be individually employed by my holding company, each receiving a salary. Added to this will be a commission of 2.5%, payable once a year, on all audited annual profits. I will explain what this means once you have accepted my proposal in principle. We will then sign a suitable contract."

Chad and Hank accepted immediately and the deal was finalised.

"Just one thing, remember my requirements of absolute anonymity and thorough due diligence before any investment is made!"

"Glenn, that is something we will never forget!"

It was only six months later that Glenn implemented his 'Resurrection Plan' and began buying again, albeit very cautiously.

"Chad, Hank, we have had 6 months to take stock of where we stand, and it is time for some cautious purchasing activity of internet investments. We are able to gage the viability of stocks from what happened in the great Market sell off and I suggest careful buying in the longer term can only mean excellent returns. In short, we should start a programme of purchasing shares in some of the world's top internet companies. We will first base our choice on annual revenue based specifics. Let's get to work." An investment plan was drawn up and put into action. Spirits were guarded but positive.

It was about a year after the bubble burst that Glenn received a call from one of his very close friends. She had been a good friend of both him and his ex-wife from quite early on in their marriage and he had over the years come to rely on everything she had to say. She was one of three women who kept Glenn updated on his children's lives.

"Glenn, I have some news for you." He knew at once it had to do with one or both of his daughters.

He had stopped trying to communicate with Hannah or her sister after the rejection of his last two letters (sent by a courier service). He had sent a total of thirty letters over the last couple of years and had subsequently turned to these friends asking them to keep him updated on the two girls. It was understood he would never divulge their names. She, as with the two others, stayed in touch with Rachel although the friendship had dwindled over time, so he was always grateful for whatever each of them had to say. They were unaware of each other's activity in keeping him informed.

"I have been told Hannah is going to be married. Isn't that wonderful news?"

"Yes, that is truly wonderful news," he happily replied. "I have sometimes wondered if they would ever marry! Hannah is over thirty years of age and it is about time she did!"

"Glenn, that is the good news. The rest is not so good. Hannah and her mother are most anxious you do not hear about it and are adamant you are not to be present in any way or form. To put it bluntly, they will not allow you anywhere near the church or reception."

"That is not a worry for me. I have had plenty of time to adjust to Rachel's bitterness and hatred. I consulted with my own General Practitioner and two Psychiatrists who both warned me of my future with the girls. I actually had no alternative but to let them go to the UK and be controlled by their mother's vindictive manipulation and mental problems. They have no need for concern. I have a lump sum set aside for Hannah's wedding but will put it back into the Stock Market or, better still, towards a new animal shelter currently under construction in Connecticut. Anyway, thank you so much for taking the time to speak to me AND all you do for me."

"It is my pleasure Glenn, take care of yourself."

Glenn stood quietly for a few minutes then put his phone back in his trouser pocket, muttering to himself.

"I always expected something like this. I knew once the reality took hold and the nightmare began to unfold that I had married a psychopath that my children would be brainwashed against me. Now I must accept the consequences. I must get on with my life and devote my time to what I am destined to do.

CHAPTER 12.

The dynamics in Glenn's office had adjusted to what he had originally envisaged. He was there most days and both Hank and Chad were part of the office contingency. There were five employees plus Glenn, so the area comfortably accommodated the entire staff.

Glenn had some time back introduced a policy of spreading the work force by outsourcing the Company Secretarial workload to professional outsiders. It had eased the internal responsibilities and helped with staff interaction and dynamics.

The general vibe was casual, but efficient and healthy. He was more than pleased. Yes, this is what he had wanted from the very beginning and felt it formed the basis of a satisfying future. He was pleased he had purchased the interleading condos in those early days and did not want to go bigger as far as office accommodation was concerned. Well, not just yet. Glenn had a vision for the years ahead.

"Hello Everybody, this is a special meeting today. I am going to outline what I consider to be the investment future for this company. Firstly, each of our three subsidiaries will be identified by a number, number 1, 2, or 3. The holding company retains it's name and Company 3 will no longer be considered a venture capital entity but an internet investment facility. The large loss in the balance sheet figures for subsidiary 3 will be used as a tax advantage situation for future investments. Hank, you and Chad are very aware that I prefer investing in recognised internet companies. My refusal to sell our Amazon holding illustrates this, so it will come as no surprise that we will be building up a presence in what we consider to be the top five internet companies on Nasdaq. I know they will recover and recover handsomely. Normality has to be resumed so normal investment principles will apply. I know much of the capital in the sector flew out the window as America lost its mind and money, but I firmly believe that the most valuable companies in the Technology sector will once again dominate Nasdaq.

The two companies we will start with in this programme are Amazon and Booking Holdings (Priceline). Amazon, as we all know, has lost large portions of its market capitalisation and Booking Holdings fell to around US$10 and, although they are higher now, they have a long way to go. Please remember we are in for the long term but at the same time caution must be exercised in each and every transaction. The internet will continue to grow, driven by commerce in general and the ever greater amounts of online information, knowledge, and of course, social networking. The rapidly increasing use of mobile devices is a major factor here. With this stabilisation, internet companies are now busy consolidating and have to make sure they gain increasing market share for dominance in their respective fields. I do not see doom and gloom and we must participate as much as possible.

"Glenn, how does this affect the other two companies?" asked Chad in his usual cold business like manner.

"You and Hank will continue in your Investment Adviser capacity, as before, plus give input on the running of the companies. Stock market daily trading will not be part of our portfolios. I will give a wider view of our activities in a minute. My presence will be on a more of a day-to-day side line level, which brings me to the second part of this meeting.

You are all aware of my interest in animal welfare and more particularly wildlife conservation. This now incorporates what I call global eco-diversity and as my focus widens so does the need to have readily available resources. Our investment policy up till now has been reinvestment of income but this is going to change. The bottom line is that you, Hank, and you Chad, will carry the responsibility to ensure the income is available at all times. We will understand this better once I get more acquainted with what I believe is the ultimate purpose in my life. We all have a purpose and I believe this is what is meant for me. Whether you are included in this is purely up to you. From now on, the administration, together with other animal welfare activities including wildlife conservation, will be part of job descriptions pertaining to all of you."

A round of clapping followed and Glenn left feeling a little awkward. He seldom said much about himself but did not regret the speech. He privately and genuinely believed this was what he was meant to do.

He once again became preoccupied with conservation matters. His experience thus far had been with Elephant and Rhino populations, and this is what he continued to investigate.

"Poaching is a widespread issue throughout Africa," he muttered ominously to himself, "and the outlook for the continent is seriously appalling."

Elephant poaching was reaching an all time high with tusks being seized in record numbers. The killing of Elephants for tusks, (Ivory), decimates South African and indeed global populations. Poaching of the Forest Elephant and the endangered African Savanah Elephant was out of control which meant that not only must the poaching stop, but co-ordinated efforts also had to be increased to stem trafficking and demand. Ivory trade had to be stopped not only in China but throughout the world. It was a dreadful scenario. He could see that knowledge sharing and proper management was a core component. Similarly with the rhino. Thinking of the Rhino he once again remembered his terrifying and deathly experience in the South African bush some years back which propelled him into action.

South Africa has the largest populations of both Elephant and Rhinos but they were fast dwindling. All six Rhino Species were on the Red List as endangered species. He contacted Dirk.

"Hello Dirk, I have not seen your reports recently. I know they are going to the Global Wildlife Partnership, as we agreed, but could you give me a quick update?" The Global Wildlife Partnership was one of the largest organisations in the world created to combat wildlife poaching and trafficking. Glenn had introduced Dirk to them and they had been working together from then on. It was an ideal relationship.

"Glenn, things are bad. Strictly between you and me, I am fighting a losing battle. Wildlife crime is rampant here in South Africa and is rife throughout the rest of the world. How are we going to put an end to this?"

"I know it is a tough fight but it has to be overcome. Are the drones as useful as we thought?"

"Yes, we couldn't do without them, and the infra-red cameras are helping us detect poachers in the dead of night." He hesitated and then continued. "I guess it is not as bad as I say. It is just the last week that has been pure hell." Glenn decided not to follow up on this last comment.

"I have been thinking," Glenn said pensively, "We should use web-based platforms to combat the illegal trade and team up with social media and e-commerce to try and implement a standardised wildlife policy framework. I see it as all about people and education. People must take care of natural resources. Forests sustain wildlife and supply people around the world with clean air, water, food and other products. People need to take care of natural resources around them," and then rather forcefully added, "Sorry I am going off at a tangent, but you can see how I am thinking. I have instituted a dot.com based investment plan which will give me some power, but it is going to take time and money to implement. Education takes time. Keep up the good work, Dirk. I will keep more in contact." It was obvious Dirk needed a break, but Glenn had no idea of how or exactly what to do.

Ideally, the way forward is to obliterate all poaching syndicates in South Africa and the rest of the world by efficient and highly trained organised forces. The necessity of a strong and determined legal system was also a factor which would be hard to find in Africa, never mind the rest of the world.

He, as he often did, began to worry about the abuse and slaughter of animal wildlife. The worry of animal life in general was catching up with him and threatening to devour all his hope and dreams for the safe and prosperous future of all animals, both land and marine. His mind wandered to thoughts of global population increases which was fuelling the ever growing demand for all wildlife and the resulting products. He thought of places like Vietnam and China where the demand for black market animal related products was astronomically high, where people are willing to pay exorbitant amounts of money for whatever they could get.

"How can wildlife conservation succeed in such a scenario," he murmured with anguish and dejection. "Glenn, pull yourself together," he moaned softly to himself, deciding then and there a fresh and tingling shower might help. The shower revitalised him and he was soon ready for his day of divergent decisions and, hopefully, positive actions. He felt it was once again time to get on with his attempts to ensure mankind united to ensure all wildlife thrives in this rapidly changing world. It was something close to his heart, something he had to do. He saw it as a sacred duty and obligation to protect all animals and wildlife for the sake of his children's future and their children, and that of all children of future generations. It would make the planet a happier and healthier place.

"Good morning GG, how are you doing this fine morning," Glenn quipped as he entered the office, "could I have a word with you in the boardroom." The sitting room in his section was also known as the boardroom by the staff and was generally used for meetings and group discussions. The two bedrooms in his condominium were kept for his use alone. The adjoining condo was strictly 'the office'. "GG, I know your views on conservation but how aware is the surfing community as a whole, on this situation?"

"Glenn, it is becoming a major matter amongst surfers. Marine life survival has become the epicentre of the surfing culture. The sea is part of a surfer's life and unsustainable practices litter the oceans with all sorts of debris, making it deadly and dangerous for surfers and all that live in the sea. Marine life faces deadly traps that mercilessly kills marine mammals, turtles and seabirds and, a growing threat to all of us who use and enjoy the sea, is the increasing abundance of ghost gear in our oceans."

"What is ghost gear?" calmly asked Glenn.

"It is abandoned objects left behind at sea and on the rocks like traps, fishing tackle and such like objects which contribute significantly to the marine problems. It is a form of marine plastic debris, damaging vital ocean habitats, aquatic life and of course livelihoods. You will be astonished at what is out there."

"I understand. Fishing feeds billions of people and is vital to the economies of countless countries and yet it is part of the aquatic turmoil the world is in. I have a feeling that the surfing community would be a sensible place to introduce a few pointers of our Marine

Conservation Programme. There is a scuba marine conservation foundation which supports ocean conservation and is doing great work in their respective area. I was reading a report of theirs about shearwater birds and the effect the plastic in maritime waters is having on them. They nest on islands around the arctic circle and fly low over the waves of the open ocean eating almost anything although their natural foods are small fish, squids and crustaceans. They however often take ship's garbage. To cut a long story short, they are dying in large numbers and virtually every dead bird has a large amount of marine plastic in it's stomach. It is frightening what is happening to our marine life in and out of the water. GG, I would like you to come up with suggestions on what we have discussed. We have to find solutions that save the incredible array of life on our planet. Saving nature is what it is all about and I believe the surfing community have a role to play in Marine Conservation. I would like you to follow up on this aspect and present me with your thoughts and recommendations. We can talk further on Thursday."

Glenn continued with his environmental education, reading whatever he could and meeting whoever would see him. It was a vast subject and although his general knowledge was growing day by day, he quickly realised a more specialised approach was an absolute necessity if he was to have any impact. He had become involved in wildlife conservation after a barbarous few months of hunting as a young man. Added to this was his passion for animal welfare. Poaching was his number one concern followed closely by Pollution. (He had recently been diagnosed with asthma which he rather stubbornly felt was the result of increasing city to city contaminated airflow). There was, however, a natural spill-over into numerous general sectors of environmental impact on the planet that also deeply concerned him. He decided to meet up with Dirk and brought forward his next trip to South Africa.

"Dirk, it is good to see you again. I am at the crossroads of my investigation of wildlife in general i.e. loss of habitat, human conflict, poaching etc. and wildlife with particular reference to certain species. Wildlife provides balance and stability to nature's processes and the aim of wildlife conservation is to ensure the survival of all earth's animals and to educate people on living sustainably with each and every species on this planet. Having said this, I think I am going forward on a species basis, which naturally leads to different countries and reactions. Does that make sense to you?"

"It certainly does Glenn but all I know about is what is happening in South Africa and, to a lesser extent, the neighbouring countries."

"I understand, and it is exactly that I want to discuss with you. A global partnership on wildlife conservation is my ultimate aim but one has to start somewhere! Please stop me where you think I might be talking irresponsibly or repeating what we have discussed before.

Let me start with the largest living animal on land, the elephant. South Africa has the largest population of elephants in Africa but they are fast dwindling, both the African bush elephant and the smaller African forest elephant. Incidentally, Botswana is home to a third of Africa's largest elephants and they are also facing severe poaching problems there. Over 90% of the original African elephant population has been wiped out in the last 80 years. Dirk, do you know that decades of ivory poaching has led to the evolution of tuskless elephants which proves that humans are literally changing the anatomy of wildlife. In the Gorongoza National Park this genetic mutation has increased dramatically. When you consider this, remember that approximately 100 African elephants are killed each day by poachers seeking ivory, meat and body parts. Furthermore, an insatiable lust for ivory products in the Asian market makes illegal ivory an extremely profitable commodity. The heartbreak of this is also the wonderful personality this animal has. They are oversized, can be bold, spiritual, protective, principled and pompous. They mourn their dead, generally feel joy, anger, grief, love, compassion, and despair. Yes, they are gentle giants helping each other in distress, and as I have said, grieve for their dead and are capable of living past 70 years old, (if mankind allows them). Dirk, we need to get this across to the people, not just of Africa but also people of the world.

I am getting carried away here but what I have to say is, I believe, vitally important. Rhino conservation is also battling to survive. Three of the five rhino species are critically endangered. Rhinos have been around for millions of years and, like the elephant, play a crucial role in their eco-system. They help shape the African landscape. They are important grazers, keeping a healthy balance in the said eco-system, but are at risk by the huge surge in poaching. They are mostly found in South Africa, Namibia, Zimbabwe and Kenya and are being killed in record numbers. You see, my friend, the work you are doing is of major importance. I won't say anymore but I reserve the right to talk about the habitat loss these two species are subject to another time. It is a topic very close to my heart."

"Glenn, give me some headers on habitat loss. I want to know more."

"Habitat destruction decreases the number of places where wildlife can live. Fragmentation breaks up a continuous tract of habitat, often dividing large wildlife plains into smaller ones. Human caused habitat loss includes deforestation, agricultural expansion and urbanisation. It increases the vulnerability of wildlife populations by reducing their space and resources and by increasing the likelihood of conflict with humans. Smaller habitats support smaller populations (herds) and smaller populations are more likely to go extinct. Having said that, you can imagine how seriously deforestation is affecting the world. The Amazon delta is testament to that."

The two men talked late into the night only managing a few hours sleep before sunrise. Two days later Glenn motored down to Hermanus, a seaside village he savoured and enjoyed. His parents kept a seaside cottage in Hermanus many years back but seldom stayed there. It was eventually sold. He never really got to enjoy the place, (it was sold when he was at University), but liked the idea of having a 'holiday home' in the village. His house in Cape Town had recently been sold so it was logical to buy a cottage next to the sea. Glenn was forever on the search for peace and believed it could be found there, in Hermanus. He had an idea in the back of his mind of either finally living in the Florida Keys or perhaps Cornwall, possibly in the St. Ives vicinity, but realised that was still far off in the future. Holidays and occasional stays in Hermanus is what it had to be for now and he found and bought a property in the Voelklip area within a week. This was his home in South Africa. The country was, in his opinion, slowly slipping into financial and political turmoil, as both he and his father had foreseen, and the future did not look too promising. Having only a cottage in the Cape and very little financial investment in South Africa as a whole, made sense. Glenn was delighted with his purchase and enjoyed two more months at the sea, after which he, together with his dogs, returned to New York. Flying with his dogs next to him was a single luxury he had always allowed himself and them. Selling the other few seats on the flight was not really as cash effective as he would have liked but the two of them being kept in an aircraft hold was not an option.

CHAPTER 13.

Historically the dot.com boom can be seen as being similar to a number of technology inspired booms of the past like railroads in the 1840's, automobiles in the early twentieth century, radio in the 1920's, TV in the 1940's, transistor electronics in the 1950's and home computers in the 1980's. Glenn had always applied logic to his investment strategy and after the dot.com boom and bust scenario, he continued applying logic to his thoughts and actions, but on a more determined level. It was time to share his latest thoughts and invited Chad and Hank into the Boardroom.

"Good Morning Gentleman, please sit down. I am constantly looking to the future spurred on by my interest and activity in wildlife conservation and related matters. You are aware that countries around world are experiencing a continually increasing problem with regard to climate change, but little is being done about it. That leads me to a man called Elon Musk. Have you heard of him?"

"I have," acknowledged Chad.

"Good, he is a South African, a Canadian and an American who was born in South Africa and now lives here in The States. I have never met him but have been following him closely. He founded PayPal which was bought by eBay a few years ago for the incredible price of$1.5 billion. Incidentally, he prescribes to the belief that for life to survive, humanity has to become a multi planet species. An interesting idea involving interplanetary travel, but it is what he is up to at present that fascinates me and has my attention. He has been long interested in electric cars and has recently become one of the major funders of Tesla Motors, an electric vehicle company founded a few years back by two entrepreneurs Martin Eberhard and Marc Tarpenning. I firmly believe this is a situation we have to watch."

"Glenn, I have to agree although I personally cannot see electric vehicles having any future," said an unimpressed Hank. Chad remained silent. "There is another side to this," continued Hank. "There are battery companies building factories as we speak, but the battery used to power electric vehicle prototypes is the extremely expensive lithium-ion battery pack and a lot more testing and development is required, added to which, is the recent slump in tech. stocks that has stripped billions of dollars in value off publicly traded battery companies. Most have no revenue because they have not begun selling a product. In my opinion the possibility of seeing electric motors replacing internal combustion engines is a very long way off. We will probably never see it."

"I appreciate your participation Hank, but you and I are looking in totally different directions. Technology is ever advancing and creating ground breaking ideas that have the potential to be revolutionary. Countries around the world are experiencing drastic changes in weather conditions with wildlife and nature in general being dramatically affected. I also understand Tesla is hard at work to create a lithium-ion battery for the electric car and possibly for smaller devices like mobiles and laptops. Climate change is one of the world's biggest challenges threatening mankind and Elon Musk could be the man to steer us out of this suffocating carbon dioxide atmosphere in which everything currently lives. It is early days and I accept it is a concept for first world luxury lifestyles, but, I firmly believe our next prime investment direction must be the electric vehicle."

Glenn wanted to continue the meeting and discuss China and what it had to offer investors but stopped himself proceeding. He had never been to China, although he was very aware of the economic reforms introduced in 1978 by the then hierarchy and recognised that there were definitely moves from initial successes in low wage sectors like clothing and footwear to more of an industrial economy, thus paving the way for a considerably more optimistic outlook for the country in general and the Shanghai and Shenzhen Stock Exchanges in particular. He would keep the Peoples Republic of China topic for another time! His obsession for a cleaner and more organised world was his priority.

Glenn had teamed up with three others to form what he called 'A likeminded collective'. It was this four that did the groundwork for what was to be the initiative for their 'Saving Nature Venture'. They all subscribed to saving nature as the very heart of conservation. All of them, other than Glenn, had previously been involved in some way with a major Conservation Organisation and all accepted that the primary way to achieve their goal was through communication and people. People had to take care of resources around them where they lived so that they could live with clean air, clean water, clean food and clean products.

"I have said before, our first step is to team up with e-commerce and social media, possibly initially through web-based platforms but all within the same area and country. Once we have a fully organised operational entity, we will move on to the next place following the same principles. It will take time, suitable employees and money. We are not talking here of a one stop scenario but of a living educational enterprise based on commercial ideas and growth. We all recognise the numerous problems within such a framework, but they are surmountable, and this can work," said Glenn with energetic enthusiasm. "By the same token our infiltration into the deadly poaching world must continue and grow. I can report that the anti-poaching progress in South Africa continues to improve, particularly Rhino, although we still have a long way to go. Nevertheless, I believe it is time to enter the other African poaching areas namely Zambia, Zimbabwe, Namibia and Kenya where we can help intensify all anti-poaching efforts. When one sees that between 1970 and 1998 around 96% of the world rhino population was lost to large scale poaching leaving a minimal total of 5000 animals, you can understand what we are up against."

"Glenn, it is looking a bit better now although I get your point," replied Mike encouragingly, "but I acknowledge we have a long way to go. One of the problems is the increasing sophisticated methods poachers use, particularly the helicopters, night vision equipment and drugs to knock them out. We need to match their level of technology alongside the efforts to reduce demand. Having said that, where do you suggest we go in next?" It was subsequently decided Namibia and Zimbabwe would be their next African anti-poaching targets with Dirk giving his thoughts and advice when required. They then turned to the ever increasing shifts in temperatures and weather patterns. It was accepted by the four of them that climate change was harming world health through air pollution, pressures on mental health and, as a result, many were suffering increased hunger and poor nutrition particularly where it was becoming near impossible for people to grow or find sufficient food.

"Fossil fuels....coal, oil and gas," continued Glenn, "account for over 75% of global greenhouse gas emissions and nearly 90% of all carbon dioxide emissions. These greenhouse emissions blanket the earth and trap the sun's heat. I do not need to remind you that the world is now warming faster than at any point in recorded history. The risks to all forms of life are mind-blowing. We just have to look at the increasing wildfires and destructive storms that are becoming more intense everywhere. Cyclones, hurricanes and typhoons feed on warmer waters and destroy homes and communities causing death and massive economic loss. Just take a look in our own back yard. Take L.A. for example. The wildfires in California are starting more easily and more frequently with thousands of homes at risk and lives shattered each time a fire takes hold. The smoke can drift hundreds of miles creating ill health whichever way it travels. I believe that seven of the largest fires in California's history have occurred in the last few years. The world must keep fossil fuels in the ground, invest in renewable energy and as you all know, my favourite topic, switch to sustainable transport!"

"We have to collaborate to reduce disaster vulnerability and that leads us back to our efforts in Education," added a determined Mike. "I see The United Nations General Assembly has actually declared 13 October of each year to be International Day for Disaster Risk Reduction. The plan is to erase awareness of the impact of natural disasters throughout the world. It also includes man-made disasters. That is where we must continue to principally operate, not forgetting of course, our new plan of extending our anti-poaching activity into Namibia and Zimbabwe."

"Absolutely," retorted Glenn, "Environmentalism is a broad philosophy and ideology that envelops environmental protection and improvement of health to humans, animals, plants and all marine life. It is in essence an attempt to balance relations between humans, animals and the various natural systems on which they depend in such a way that all components are accorded a proper degree of sustainability. I think we have a realistic plan on the way forward."

"Don't get too technical Glenn, keep it simple," added Mike laughing. He was very aware of the passion that rumbled inside his friend's body. Sometimes it needed to be controlled.

All agreed and accepted that current programmes would remain in place and dispersed. The world had to go forward urgently to survive. Implementation of their programme had begun.

CHAPTER 14.

Glenn had grown to enjoy New York and what it had to offer. His living accommodation had turned out to be limited but suitable in many ways. Chelsea, on the West Side of Manhattan was fast becoming an art district and he would spend many hours wandering the numerous galleries viewing work done by both established and emerging artists. He had a reasonable collection of art in South Africa, (he had sold some pieces when he moved his belongings to the Hermanus house) and found himself buying a few new works for the New York apartment and the office. He spent many hours walking, running and cycling in trendy attractions like the High Line, an elevated park built over an historic former freight rail line, elevated above the streets of West Side Manhattan. He considered it to be one of Manhattan's outdoor gems although it was rapidly attracting an increasing number of people. It was about one and a half miles long but, regrettably for him, was growing in popularity. He had to admit it was a wonderful outdoor attraction and a great urban trail, but he did like his own space. He generally used it weekdays only. He was also a very keen swimmer and could be found most days training either in the McBurney YMCA pool or the Chelsea Piers Fitness pool. Added to this were the numerous dog parks throughout Manhattan which his dogs seriously enjoyed. Glenn had noted their social skills had improved enormously! They certainly loved what the city had to offer. In spite of all this, when November arrived both he and the dogs were always ready for hotter climates and Hermanus was the never-ending choice.

Once again, the South African summer season was fast approaching and it was time to pack a few summer essentials and take to the skies.

Glenn settled in to his Hermanus house hoping to find relaxation and quiet. It would not happen. His mind was it's own master and no matter how hard he fought he found himself surveying deepest dark Africa. Although it was only his mind playing games, he was consumed by everything that was climate Change. He felt The Like-Minded Collective was not achieving enough. He would have to take control.

"What are the effects of climate control?" he asked himself.

Hotter temperatures….as greenhouse gas concentrates rise so does the global surface temperature.

More severe storms develop.

Increased drought becomes common place.

A warming and rising ocean is the result.

The loss of animal species.

Not enough food.

More health risks.

Spread of certain diseases.

Poverty and displacement.

Climate change will impact human health with worsening air and water quality.

This led him on to think of how he and his fellow colleagues might help stop the ever threatening advancement of climate change.

Everyone must reduce their personal impact on the climate crises.

Speaking out and influencing those around us must be immediate.

If we act now, we can save the planet.

Power homes with renewable energy and have energy efficient appliances.

Reduce water waste.

Solar panelling.

He continued muttering to himself.

"If we do not start now, the wildlife we so love will find their habitat destroyed leading to mass extinction. Agriculture will plummet. The reality is it affects all of us. I just hope I am correct in thinking we still have time to limit the worst of the impact. WE MUST WORK TOGETHER. I must get this across."

He knew there was much more to be considered but, at last, felt his head slipping into his chest and he fell asleep.

Glenn suddenly woke up, checked the time and opened up his email on his mobile. Starring at it through groggy eyes, he saw an email from his daughter Hannah. They had not been in contact since before her wedding.

"What could she possibly want?" he whispered to himself, opened it up and read, "We will be in Cape Town in three weeks staying in a Guest House in Upper Tamboerskloof. Maybe we can meet up?"

Glenn decided to leave his reply until the morning. Matters of climate change, the electric vehicle industry, Wall Street, and whether to invest in the Chinese market, had all lately been playing havoc with his mind and now Hannah had joined them. He seriously needed rest. He knew prayer would help him sort it out and went back to bed.

That morning he made a decision. He was going to reply to his daughter with a time and place to meet and that would be 'it' for the next few weeks. He simply was doing nothing else but rest and enjoy Hermanus.

"Best decision I have ever made," he quietly said to himself.

Hannah and her husband met with him a few weeks later over lunch which turned out to be an interesting get-together. He was fully aware of his ex-wife's many efforts at destroying his children's relationship with their father and during the lunch he was totally normal and in no way self serving, neither in speech or manner. The wedding was never mentioned, nor would it ever be.

Glenn spent many months in Hermanus enjoying the summer but was constantly online with the New York office. GG, his personal assistant and Office Manager, had been one of his business's success stories. Glenn found himself relying on him more and more in all matters, particularly relating to his business affairs, but also appreciated his efforts in other areas. GG. had become his guide and advisor on many matters although never on business moves and decisions. Glenn listened to what his colleagues generally had to offer but the final decision was always taken by him alone.

It was on these South African stays that he would examine the country's progress, (if any), in both the anti-poaching arena and conservation in general. He particularly looked at youth education in the hope that an increasingly comprehensive approach to climate change was happening on all levels of formal education. It was imperative it included wildlife conservation. The reason for this was he wanted to know if support and climate change resources, (which obviously included him albeit in a very minor role), was reaching the teachers and activists and to ensure that the recipients were well informed and equipped to face climate change challenges. His intention from the beginning was to create an interdisciplinary approach to climate change/wildlife education on all levels of the formal education sector and he wanted to ensure it was included in subjects such as business studies and languages. It was a formidable project which he alone had no hope of handling but a little 'Pushing' could only help! His big worry was the so-called cultural habit of discarding paper, plastic and similar waste literally where the individual stood or walked. It seemed to be a growing problem in many parts of the world, particularly in third world lifestyles where the discarded waste often ended up in rivers and oceans. It was a major factor for the rapidly declining marine life habitat.

Soon, the Cape chilly winds were felt with winter not far behind signalling the imminent return to the States. Glenn had a lot on his mind and was eager to be in Manhattan once again. The thought of pool swimming again also appealed. His morning open water sessions in the ocean at Hermanus were not in the same league! He had always acknowledged to himself that he was not really an open water swimmer of any merit.

CHAPTER 15.

Glenn had developed a strong interest in the developing Electric Car Industry once he realised that the harmful emissions from automobile traffic could be substantially reduced if they were to replace fossil fuel powered vehicles. The world was already seeing the loss of, sea ice, melting glaciers, a sea level rise and more intense heat waves, all due to climate change. It was common knowledge that global temperature increases, from human made greenhouse gases, would continue and that severe weather damage was to increase and intensify and yet, the same 'world' was being extremely slow to accept the electric vehicle. Technology was ever advancing creating ground breaking ideas which have the potential to be revolutionary. There had to be a surge in EV production and popularity. Glenn was mesmerised but, as he saw it, there was one problem, the battery. If this weakness could be overcome there was no end in sight for electric cars. Electric motors work much more efficiently than internal combustion engines. They are faster and can produce high torque from standing. There were no moving parts and no changing oil routines, resulting in much lower maintenance costs. The only draw-back was the battery. Glenn was intrigued but not overwhelmed by all that was the electric car. Whether to invest in the industry or not, never arose. He was a total EV believer. Then he came across a remarkable man called Elon Musk. Tesla had been incorporated in 2003 and he had joined the company in 2004 putting in $6.3 million of the company's $6.5 million share capital. He subsequently became Tesla's Chairman. Later the electric automaker went public at $17 a share and soon after, it's model S officially went on sale. In the same year the model MX with gullwing doors also became available. Glenn started buying into the company.

"Good morning Everybody, I have asked you all to join me in the boardroom today. As you know I am very much in favour of our investing in the electric motor vehicle industry. I believe the time has come to start the process. We will not require our usual investment investigations that I normally insist upon, so please take what I have to say as 'the initial purchase being approved'. Our entry is to be slow and calculated and please remember the requirement of ANONYMITY.

The Tesla Company is in its early stages but we have to start somewhere so it might as well be now."

Soon after this initial purchase, problems developed. Production delays combined with the millions of dollars Tesla burned every year suddenly sent the stock crashing. Glenn kept buying. He was very aware that there was a growing outcry concerning the battery being too expensive and not practical, but they were forgetting that Tesla had already effectively created the electric vehicle battery industry and that people were willing to buy electric vehicles thus forcing advanced electric battery manufacturers from their laboratories into mass production. Producing battery cells by the millions in a factory is vastly different to making a few hundred in a clean room. Elon musk had proved that next generation battery cells could be produced and Tesla had already proved that their batteries were safe and reliable. (As previously mentioned, they were hard at work to create an alternative which would revolutionise smaller devices such as laptops and mobiles). The electric vehicle could compete with fossil fuel powered vehicles for convenience and price and at the same time substantially reduce harmful emissions from automobile traffic. Glenn saw a future for effective climate control and all that went with it. He no longer just imagined a world where one would plug cars into solar panels and wind turbines. It was clear to him now that it was soon to be the everyday reality and that domestic solar systems and electric vehicles were a perfect match. He continued to buy Tesla shares. More and more Tesla cars were seen on the roads even though they were not good on long trips. They were hampered by the lack of power stations if and when they went outside the estimated mileage zone. He was confidant Elon Musk was pushing his employees and Panasonic, Tesla's battery manufacturer, to overcome the difficulties. Panasonic had the ability to handle the advanced requirements of Tesla technology and with new battery technology were continually lowering the lithium-ion battery pack cost to the consumer. It was becoming smaller, cheaper and even lighter.

"Good Morning Everybody," greeted Glenn, as per usual when addressing an investment meeting. "I want to draw your attention to two interesting topics that are open for discussion today. You are all familiar with our current activity on Wall Street and I propose the following for our consideration. Many publicly traded battery companies were stripped of millions of dollars in value during the slump in Technology Stocks with most of them not having any revenue because they had not begun selling a product. Producing battery cells by the millions is vastly different to making a few hundred in a small space designed to minimise contaminants. I believe we should look into the scenario and see if there is any benefit investing in this sector. It is only a thought at this stage although I do see a surge in production and with technology ever advancing and creating ground breaking ideas, there has to be potential for revolutionary advancement of some kind. Do you agree?"

"Very much so," Hank said nodding his head. There was full agreement.

"The next matter I want to mention is the increasing demand in Europe and China. China is the world's biggest market for electric vehicles and they are well behind the United States. I see electric vehicles going massively public all over the world, not only in cars but also in two and three wheelers, buses and trucks. Included in this are delivery fleets, police vehicles etc. etc. The mind boggles when one considers Tesla's lead in the electric vehicle area."

Chad and Hank were dumb founded. They recognised the possibilities were enormous but Glenn could see some hesitation. He knew they both sometimes worried about his sanity! He enjoyed playing on their thoughts but this time he had been totally serious. He would have liked to know Elon Musk's views!

Suddenly, out of the blue, Elon Musk claimed he had secured funding for $420 per Tesla share, a significant premium at the time. The Securities and Exchange Commission accused Musk of fraud. He paid a $20million fine while Tesla paid a separate $20million fine. In spite of this Glenn continued with the purchasing programme but, like his employees, also began to question his sanity! He, during his investigations, had come to know about a small company called Rivian, an American electric vehicle automaker building an electric sport utility and a pick-up truck. He began to silently watch it with interest. Also around this time he had, by pure chance, found out more about Elon Musk the man.

A habit he had acquired years ago was having a cooked egg and toast breakfast, (he had never taken to the American sweet taste preference), and generally chose one of the many coffee houses in his area of Manhattan to do so. There was one particular coffee house he favoured and happened to develop a 'Good Morning' chat with one of the servers. They were soon on first name terms.

"Good Morning David, are you well today?"

"A bit tired but relaxed enough," came the reply. "I worked the late shift and got to sleep well after midnight, but I must admit I enjoy my job."

"Might I say you are very good at it. Do you have any plans for the future?"

"Not really. Have you ever heard of Elon Musk?"

"Indeed, I have and must admit to being a fan of his, why do you ask?"

Now Glenn was interested!

David went on tell the incredible story of him and, many servers like him, each having amassed around a million dollars or more in buying Tesla shares.

"There is a whole group of us, and I am pretty sure many others, who follow every move he makes, and it has paid off. Each month I buy a few more Tesla shares. I put as much as I can afford into the stock and it all comes from this job. I love my work although I never need to work again! Elon Musk is a legend. He dedicates himself to what he does sometimes working a 20 hour day." Then he let slip something that intrigued Glenn. "He is incredibly high functioning and gets fixated on specific things. I guess that comes from him having Asperger's Syndrome but he certainly sees the world in a unique way." Glenn added a few pleasantries and left for the office. He intended to find out about Asperger's Syndrome. He had never heard of it before and took him two days to fully understand.

1. Accurate diagnosis is sometimes difficult.

2. They have above normal intelligence and a significant percentage exhibit extraordinary abilities.

3. They have extremely sharp memories and instinctively grasp difficult concepts.

4. They can commit to memory huge amounts of information and knowledge about selective interests.

5. They come across as obsessively self-absorbed and are concerned only about things that interest them.

6. They normally have a narrow field of interest with savant like understanding.

Glenn felt he finally understood what made Elon Musk the success he was but never discussed what he believed to be true with anyone. He continued to buy Tesla stock but on a very selective basis.

Price and the amount of available cash were the two overriding factors but more important to him was the planned development of mega factories worldwide, not only for Tesla cars but also lithium-ion batteries, solar shingles, chargers and other related production parts. In addition to this was Musk's SpaceX space exploration company through which he had gained worldwide attention for a series of historic milestones such as being capable of returning a spacecraft from low-earth orbit, and the building of the Dragon Spacecraft which became the first commercial way of delivering cargo to and from the International Space Station. He had achieved this while making a more affordable re-usable rocket. Glenn recognised his brilliance but now thought he had a greater understanding of Elon Musk, the man with the advantage of Asperges Syndrome tendencies.

Glenn felt he could now take things a little easier and get back into enjoying New York. He was mistaken.

His phone rang early one morning, it was Dirk in South Africa.

"Hello Glenn, I hope you are well. Do you have a few minutes for me?" His voice was brittle and he sounded disturbingly distracted.

"Of course I do."

"There are two matters I want to discuss with you. The first is actually beyond comprehension. I went up with my girlfriend to the Limpopo region for a four day getaway. On the last day our guide said he had something to show us."

"What was that?" enquired Glenn calmly and politely.

"We heard distant screeching and immediately made our way towards the area it came from. The nearer we got the more unbearable was the sound. It was one of the most toxic sights imaginable, and you know what I normally come across daily in my line of work! Five people were randomly hammering the skulls of donkeys that surrounded them. These animals were aimlessly being beaten to death. Homemade hammers were the death weapons. You would never have believed human beings could show such violence and blood thirsty pleasure towards any animal. I felt their pain inside me. Their shrill screams of anguish and fear was too much and I completely lost control. The worst part, when the hammering of their skulls did not kill, was the skinning of the donkeys alive. I was told it was part of a well-orchestrated campaign in the rampant breeding, poaching, slaughtering and exporting of donkey parts to China. Glenn we have to do something about this! It must be stopped."

"This is absolutely appalling. Leave it with me and I will see what I can do. What is the other matter you want to discuss?"

"My heart is one hundred percent in my job but honestly, I don't know how much more I can take of the cruelty and brutal destruction of animal wildlife. I see beating, shooting, stabbing and abuse on a daily basis and cannot take it anymore. Have you not got something for me in New York. I am in a serious relationship and I have to think about her future as well."

"I understand where you are coming from Dirk. Let me think about what you say and make some enquiries. Leave it with me."

"I cannot thank you enough my friend."

Glenn knew this had been coming and had dreaded the day it was to happen. Dirk was a special man and had to be looked after. He also knew it was to have a major effect on his own anti-poaching involvement even though it was from New York. He was aware that some broader-based poaching measures in South Africa achieved only limited success in disrupting illegal wildlife markets and poaching in general. The Black Mambas, groups of women, had fairly recently been created to form units of female wildlife rangers in various recognised danger areas and were having a marked effect on the individual local wildlife poaching problem. Dirk had used a direct, more deadly approach, and definitely had a high success rate. With him gone, tactics would have to be changed for a more recognised approach and would become a whole new ball game, way beyond control from New York. He felt trapped. His participation in anti-poaching in that country had to come to an end. The Amazon coupled with climate change would now have his attention but his business interests came first. For the first time in his 'Buying Tesla" campaign he was having doubts about the company and its production plans. He knew there was the construction of massive Tesla factories, (Giga Factories), planned in Texas, Shanghai, (earmarked as the main export hub to Europe), and Berlin signalling a huge increase in global vehicle production which would allow it to achieve new record output. He was worried that the figures given were a little too optimistic. Did they have a balance point between supply and demand?

His uncertainty left only one choice, the halt in further purchases.

"Hank, I know you have been concerned about Tesla from the word go so will not be surprised by my placing a stop on purchases for the moment. We have a substantial holding but, viewed against our other two shareholding portfolios, it is not a disproportionate figure and our profit margins are huge. Enough said."

"Yes Glenn, and I am the only one in the office who has not been personally buying Tesla shares!"

"They still have a long way to go but I feel a breather is necessary to review all aspects. You will become a buyer somewhere along the line," Glenn laughingly replied.

The office routine became quieter once again and everyone slowly began to relax. Then, the bombshell hit Glenn.

"Good morning everyone," said GG. coughing painfully as he entered. He then casually whispered to Glenn. "Can we talk privately?"

The two men went to the boardroom and closed the door.

"GG. you look a little tired. What can I do for you?"

"I have to tell you something in confidence. I received some worrying news yesterday which I need to share with you. I have been feeling rather weak and fatigued these last few months and on top of that experiencing pain and persistent tummy troubles. It has steadily got worse with breathing difficulties and chronic headaches, so last week I went to my local doctor. The prognosis is not good. I have stage four colon cancer. I have two to three months left."

Glenn put his arms around him and the two momentarily stood still. GG. burst into tears as Glenn wiped a tear from his own eyes. It was devastating to say the least.

"I am here for you, we can beat this," said Glenn feeling a jumble of helpless emotions overpowering him.

"No I cannot," moaned GG. "I had to tell you first. I am going to tell my wife this evening although I wish I could keep it from her. I don't want to cause her any pain. Dear God I know what pain is. Please forgive me but I have to get back home. I am not ready to share this with the office yet."

Glenn looked at him gently. "I am here for you 24 hours if you need me. My time is one hundred percent yours." He saw the terrible distress in his dear friend and colleague's face. He was shocked and devastated.

GG. died six weeks later. A memorial service was held in nearby St. Peter's Episcopal Church arranged by Glenn and attended by GG's family and friends, many of whom were fellow surfers. He had been an integral part of the office as well as handling Glenn's personal affairs plus a remarkable friend. His death was a major upset to all who knew him.

"Hello everybody, we are experiencing a sad and difficult time leaving us with a lot to handle both physically and mentally. GG. did so much for the office but we have to take over and go forward, so please, let us concentrate on keeping the office wheel's turning and take each day as it comes for the moment. I just need to fathom where we are going. Circumstances have changed and I will speak to each one of you to get your individual thoughts and ideas. We will not be replacing GG. immediately." With that he murmured to Hank, "could we talk?" and went into the boardroom.

"Hi Hank, I want to sound you out on my going to Hermanus in a week or two. Can you manage the new situation without GG? I am sorely going to miss him as far as helping me with personal matters, I can adjust but what about the general running of the office and so on?"

"We will be fine as long as I can get hold of you if need be. There is a rumour regarding a split in Tesla stock but that is, as I say, probably a rumour."

"Talking of Tesla shares, I want you to watch for any information on the unlisted Rivian Organisation. I have established that a Saudi Arabian, Abdul Latif Jameel, is a part owner, (his family company has a presence in many countries), and I think Amazon and Ford are in it too. If I am correct Amazon owns 18 %, Ford 11% and Jameel 12%, so through our Amazon holding we do have an interest. It is a well run American transport and passenger vehicle company with headquarters in California and a manufacturing plant in Illinois. The electric vehicle side was started in 2009, and, so I have been told, their electric pick-up truck design is extra special and will in all probability, seriously appeal to the market. I have been watching the company but there are no signs of an impending Wall Street listing. Please keep tabs on it. I expressly want to be informed of any test drives."

"Yes, it is on our list as you requested." The two discussed other office matters and Hank left.

Glenn sat back and murmured, "I need some soothing peace in an environment of serene tranquillity. Hermanus here I come. Hopefully that means no unnecessary emails and phone calls from Manhattan."

CHAPTER 16.

Hermanus was always a place of seclusion and relaxation for Glenn. His house was one street away from Grotto Beach so early morning swims were the norm, after which it was a coffee and toast breakfast. The dogs enjoyed their first meal of the day before also going down to the beach. He would then settle into his writing. Countdown to Corruption was essentially a fictitious story built up around Charlie Hall, a young Englishman, and his business associates, living in South Africa. The reader finds him or herself transported through a hub of terror, crime, rampant decimation of wildlife and increasing discontent with the plot encompassing highly controversial solutions to Africa's problems, all of which Glenn firmly attributed to what was the reality of South Africa at the time of writing this novel. He was half way through writing and was trying to complete it during his stay in Hermanus. He enjoyed the creativity of writing and had earlier on in his life occasionally written for two or three European and American financial publications. The plan was to allot at least two hours a day to the project. It was early winter so the time frame was certainly possible and he quickly settled in to the routine.

He then struck a problem totally manufactured by him alone. He noticed all the houses around him were uninhabited. They were holiday homes showing no sign of life for the winter months and safety began to haunt him. This was the first time in his life he had actually been concerned about his security and safety. He would think he was being ridiculous and stay calm and unperturbed for a few weeks and then, once again, suddenly switch back to the alert mode. It was not a way to live. Fortunately he had purchased a plot in a security estate a few years back thinking he might build a holiday house for two of his grandchildren. He put his house up for sale and started building a cottage on the plot. The plan was he would build and live in it for a few years with the idea of eventually going to The Florida Keys or somewhere near St. Ives in Cornwall. In theory it was a good plan, but the property market was struggling, and he could not sell the Voelklip house. The holiday cottage was near completion requiring his daily presence, so he chose to move in, the prime reason being safety for himself and his belongings. It was the second house to be built within the estate and two instances of building material theft had occurred which meant he had no choice. It took another 10 months before the Voelklip holiday house was sold. In between the packing and moving Glenn completed his current novel. Sales were slow to start but steadily grew. Emphasis on sales was then directed towards the wildlife market and it's holding institutions. It became a great success selling in the USA, Europe, Russia, India and Japan. A Chinese publishing house approached Glenn with a proposal for translation, publishing rights, and entry into the Chinese market which he naturally refused. Dogs and cats were part of his life blood and he simply could not allow the book to be sold in China. He was criticised by many..... it was a very personal decision. He recognised that China was one of the world's foremost economic powers but always hesitated when considering an investment. The Economic reforms from 1978 onwards helped the country to achieve this accolade and was considered to be the world's next Silicon Valley. He however had always thought the government overstated the economic figures and thus the growth rate year on year. In 2016 his thoughts were confirmed in an article, claiming the Chinese economy had been overstated by between twelve and sixteen percent. A subsequent article said that more than half of the economists consulted, claimed a growth rate in the five to seven percent range. Nevertheless, like Japan and Korea, the Chinese economy had rapidly rising income levels and living standards while producing goods that were consumed globally. They had to be doing something right. Glenn was impressed but still hesitated even though it was now an industrial powerhouse having moved beyond success in low-wage sectors like clothing and footwear to sophisticated production of computers, pharmaceuticals and cars. Was he missing out on some ingrown prejudice? The dog and cat eating syndrome by the Chinese could not be ignored. The Shenzhen stock Exchange was continually showing an increasing optimism, in many instances a faster upward movement than most other markets around the world but he was not bothered by appearing prejudicial and ignorant. Even though China was one of the world's most foremost economic powers, he would not be investing in the country.

Glenn decided nothing was to be modified with his climate change activity or his investment portfolio programme. He did however want to spend more time in Hermanus and set up a system whereby he could do so.

It was during this period that an extraordinary meeting took place. Glenn was an habitual church goer with a set service schedule and a standard pew sitting position for most Sundays. One Sunday morning he took his seat as per normal waiting for the service to begin. Casually, out of the corner of his eye he noticed an extremely beautiful young lady walking past him time and time again. Glenn thought nothing of it until she sat down behind him. She then tapped him on the shoulder and asked.

"Are you by any chance Glenn Kirk?"

"Yes indeed I am," Glenn replied to discover she was the daughter of a very good family friend. It did not end there. Hayley Schonborn was with her mother Annie at St.Peter's! He had last seen mother and daughter during their visit to his Umdloti home some thirty years back. Glenn and Annie had been friends from their teenage years, first meeting when she visited her cousin at St. John's College. Furthermore, the two of them, plus Carl her husband, had been friends at University! In addition to all this, Annie was his daughter's Godmother. Little did they ever expect to meet up in Hermanus or that they would end up publishing Annie's biography together. This illustrates how small the modern world really is. An addition to this event was Glenn meeting Roz. Lindbergh, a neighbour of the Schonborn's. Roz's maiden name was Kirk. She asked him if there could be a family link but Glenn assured her not, only to discover a few years later that Roz's Grandfather and his Great-Grandfather were one and the same person!

The reality of the longer Hermanus stays resulted in Glenn using social media on a far greater level with spending less and less time in New York. Then Covid hit the world. He could not be apart from Harry, his now only English Springer Spaniel, and the two of them became grounded in South Africa. Fortunately, his daughter Hannah and family who had been in the country for a short holiday, returned to the United Kingdom a few days before the Covid international restrictions became law. The severity of the resulting pandemic displayed all signs of an acute global emergency and movement between the USA and

South Africa came to a halt. It was premature but, Glenn had to start setting up plans for himself and his financial investments future. The so-called retirement future had been, more or less, planned around him choosing to live in Cornwall or The Florida Keys. He had naturally visited both a number of times but had never developed a base in either one. This did not worry him. His chief concern was his deep involvement in the wildlife conservation which, by necessity included climate change. When he analysed his involvement in protecting populations of some of the world's most ecologically and culturally important species, he had to admit survival was the driving force behind his initiative. Loss of habitat was part of it but it was wildlife conservation that drew him into the climate change arena. It was all part of the whole and had to be treated as such. He was, and had been most of his life, totally committed. His early life and the disastrous toxic marriage had been for a reason and this reason had to go forward after his death. It would take time but he knew what he had to do. Covid isolation would be turned into an opportunity. He set about reading up on all aspects of climate change related to the Amazon and its forests.

He had long known that habitat destruction interacts with climate change and that the Amazon was very much a case in point. The Amazonian forests were dying and being progressively replaced by brush and savannah-like grasslands and there was a serious threat of about 55% of the Amazon rainforest being severely damaged by 2030, a dire future for humans, animals and the rainforests. This in turn causes increased erosion, decreased agricultural yields, greater insect infestation and spread of infectious diseases. Glenn was appalled on what he discovered knowing that increased temperatures and changing rain patterns would seriously affect the regions water availability, rain patterns, agriculture and the inhabitant's health. About 50% of The Amazon rainforest could be converted into dry savannah which would viciously impact on the wildlife. He found this too frightening to contemplate but he did write numerous emails to relevant individuals and organisations voicing his concern.

"I will need another life time to fight this," he mumbled to himself. "My loyalty and future efforts must be with what I originally started, wildlife and animal welfare. I realise there is a serious risk of losing a large part of the Amazonian forests and, if warming goes up by just a few degrees, the process of more bush and savannah like grasslands developing will become irreversible. The Amazon will become a major source of carbon dioxide. I am too old to participate in fighting this." For the first time in his life he felt his age.

CHAPTER 17.

Covid was sweeping the world with its calculated infected microscopic pores. The world introduced isolation for all villages, towns, cities, countries and continents, but unavoidably, the pandemic triggered a freefall in share prices. Social media thrived. Glenn found running his investment business in The States while sitting at his computer in South Africa came easily to him and visa versa so did his colleagues, but the world had changed transforming lives, economies and the fortunes of most businesses. Prices fluctuated although the fundamental trends accelerated, propelling some companies forward at record speeds while other's found their headwinds turning into hurricanes. The first month saw large and rapid declines but the duration was relatively short as governments started to respond with record stimulus packages. Glenn simply watched from the side-lines as he noted some sectors recover. Pharmaceuticals were an obvious buy as were on-line shopping, digital entertainment, e-commerce and remote learning stocks, but he lacked his usual enthusiasm and did nothing. He thought a great deal about his son who had been literally obliterated by the sick and demented Rachel. 'What could have been' played havoc with his mind and soul, but he knew what he had achieved, although relatively minor when compared with the five major international players, it was nevertheless part of a life-saving exercise for wildlife and the world. He knew he should have some pride but somehow it had never been in his nature to acknowledge it. Pride had never been part of his vocabulary. It was time to follow through with all the groundwork and systems he had set up over the years. Glenn arranged a special house-sitting environment in Constantia, Cape Town, for his beloved dog Harry and flew directly to New York. He planned to be away for two weeks.

It was an exceedingly busy time for Glenn with giving instructions and finalising the way forward for everything that had been achieved since the days of his setting up his business operation in New York. He had given much thought about the future and realised what he had achieved needed to take on a new identity and growth pattern. There had been a remarkable interest among the climate change/wildlife business community but he felt the selective portfolio investments plus very strong cash reserves were behind the attention. Glenn was looking for commitment, experience and vision. Numerous meetings had been organised prior to him arriving and all seemed to be going particularly well. Then suddenly, out of the blue, he received a call from Cape Town.

Harry was suffering extreme anxiety, not eating and generally showing signs of illness. Glenn caught the next plane out of JFK and flew back to Cape Town. He had only been in New York for six days. Harry looked terrible but was beside himself with joy and the two of them motored back to Hermanus. Glenn soon recovered from the exhausting flight and vowed he would never leave his treasured boy ever again.

Future short New York business meetings would be held in Hermanus, South Africa, and he would make a one or two month visit to New York each year with Harry in tow at his side. He still had not firmly decided on his place of residence for his final years but, due to his disastrous family scenario, he was determined it would never be possible for his ex-wife Rachel to benefit in any way whatsoever from his American Living Legacy. A business plan was slowly forming in his brain and finally he knew exactly what he should do. He had always had a masterplan in place from the very beginning but had never imagined the outcome of the American part of his life would be the success it turned out to be. How wonderful it would have been if he could have shared it with his father and mentor, Albert Edward Kirk.

Glenn had no doubt father and son would meet again.

EPILOGUE

It is a great world we live in but much is needed to prevent the inevitable decay and ever present loss of life. I see some hope as people become more responsibly aware and, in some small way, I like to think I have been party to this awareness. I, in a very limited way, see a forward movement in the worlds growing population towards a greater understanding of the life saving action that so desperately needs to be implemented. The groundwork initiated by me and my colleagues continues.

I am presently in Hermanus in the Western Cape, South Africa, and continue to be undecided about my final place of residence for the coming years. I suspect it will be Cornwall but I have no existing foundation of friends or any support group in the area and my age is suddenly becoming a major factor. Old age is something I simply do not understand but am totally aware that I need to realise its trials and its inadequacies. Hermanus has been a pleasure many times during the course of my life and a place of refuge and delight when I needed it. It also provides me with all the solitude I desire and feeds my continuing appetite for my own company. I have one very strong wish, and that is to live longer than my ever faithful and wonderful dog, Harry, and know that once he has gone I can let myself go and be with him in another place.

Yes, maybe Hermanus is where I should remain.

Ingram Content Group UK Ltd.
Milton Keynes UK
UKHW050259150523
421713UK00018B/59

9 780639 760027